IDEAPRESS
PUBLISHING

Published by Ideapress Publishing. **Ideapress Publishing** |
www.ideapresspublishing.com
All trademarks are the property of their respective companies.

Design by Duarte, Inc.

Cataloging in publication data is on file with the Library of Congress.
ISBN: 978-1-940858982

Printed in Canada

SPECIAL SALES
Ideapress Books are available at a special discount for bulk purchases,
for sales promotions and premiums, or for use in corporate training
programs. Special editions, including personalized covers, a custom
foreword, corporate imprints, and bonus content are also available.

Data
Story

EXPLAIN DATA AND
INSPIRE ACTION
THROUGH STORY

by Nancy Duarte

To the great One.

Praise for Duarte DataStory™

"Much of the disruption today is driven by data. By combining storytelling with data, you'll be better equipped to lead."
Charlene Li, author of *The Disruption Mindset* and the *New York Times* best seller, *Open Leadership*

"*DataStory* is a roadmap for anyone who works with data and struggles to bridge the precarious chasm between exploring data and explaining data."
Zach Gemignani, CEO, Juice Analytics, author of *Data Fluency*

"Duarte recognizes and taps into our real, human desire for storytelling, even when you're dealing with data. In *DataStory*, as always, Duarte inspires while she's teaching in her inimitable way."
Scott Berinato, author of *Good Charts* and the *Good Charts Workbook*

"As usual, I watched Nancy throw everything she had into writing this book. *DataStory* is probably the best work she's done so far. What's most amazing to me, though, is where she finds the time to be an incredible wife, run a firm, and write. A truly remarkable work from an equally remarkable woman."
Mark Duarte, doting husband and father of her children

Data
Story

**EXPLAIN DATA AND
INSPIRE ACTION
THROUGH STORY**

Table of Contents

SECTION 3 | MAKE CLEAR CHARTS AND SLIDES

A Slidedoc is a dense slide intended to be read, not presented.

INTRODUCTION

Understand the Science of Story

Storytelling makes the brain light up in a way no other form of communication does. Now that scientists have studied the brain while a story is being told, they can measure and map brain activity.

STORIES ENGAGE OUR SENSES

Stories engage the brain at all levels: intuitive, emotional, rational, and somatic. When we hear stories, our brains respond by making sense of information more completely. Once engaged, the limbic system (the emotional part of the brain) releases chemicals that stimulate feelings of reward and connection. Stories trigger Broca's area (language processing) and Wernicke's area (language comprehension). The trigger travels until it has made its way through the motor cortex, auditory cortex, olfactory cortex, visual cortex, shared memory, and amygdala.[1]

When we find ourselves hooked to a particular storyline, that resonance begins in our brains. This is the first trigger to enabling a physical and emotional response.

STORIES BRING US CLOSER TOGETHER

Spoken narrative creates a powerful connection between the storyteller and the listener. Thoughts, brain activations, and behaviors become synchronized, causing our brains to literally "tick together." When we exchange stories, we build a common ground of experience. The emotion infused into the spoken word is a mighty tool that melds our minds and brings our emotions into greater alignment.[2]

If you've ever felt a wave of emotion while listening to a story, that's because our brains are naturally activated and eager to physically process the emotion associated with oral description.

STORIES MOVE US TO FEEL

Stories have the magical ability to fully immerse listeners, making them feel like they have been transported into the narrative. When we are mentally stimulated by stories, our attention shifts away from critical thinking and becomes distracted by positive feelings. On the other hand, when we process things analytically, we are prone to more critical thoughts and fewer positive feelings. Product ads that use stories allow consumers to imagine themselves using the product and getting its benefits, which persuades them that they want it.[3]

Giving your audience a vicarious thrill puts them at the center of your story, making them feel like they are the hero themselves.

STORIES MOVE US TO ACT

The responses enacted by our brains can elicit a sense of empathy, urgency, or even great affliction. In a study that had people listen to a story about a father's relationship with his young, dying son, the neural responses of participants were measured, and two emotions were found to have been felt strongly amongst them: distress and empathy. Participants were monitored before and after they heard the story, and the result showed spikes in cortisol, which focuses our attention, and oxytocin, which is connected with empathy. The most astounding finding was that narratives can compel us into action by physically altering the chemistry in our brains.[4]

Stories that capture our attention cause us to emotionally connect with others and feel motivated to embark on a course of action.

Transform Numbers into Narratives

Empathy is the DNA of our work at Duarte, Inc., and story is the method used to engage hearts and spur action. In these pages, I share techniques for communicating data in the form of a story. Data doesn't speak for itself; it needs a storyteller.

With prolific digital devices and technological advancements, every person, place, thing, or idea can be measured and tracked in some way. But without identifying the story emerging from the data, it's of little to no value. Why is storytelling so important? Because the human brain is wired to process stories. By transforming your data into vivid scenes and structuring your delivery in the shape of a story, you will make your audience care about what your data says.

In the book *Made to Stick*, Chip and Dan Heath cite an experiment Chip conducted with his Stanford class that tested the memorability of facts versus stories. Students had to give a one-minute speech about crime using statistics he provided. "In the average one-minute speech," the authors share, "the typical student used 2.5 statistics. Only one student in ten told a story." In the next part of the study, students were asked to recall the speeches. While a mere five percent of them could remember a specific statistic, 63 percent remembered the stories.[5] Students could recall the stories because their emotions were activated.

In a book about communicating data, how do I define story? I'll start by stating what it's not. We're not asking you to embrace fairy tales or incorporate any sort of creative fiction into your data process. Instead, you'll utilize stories with a structure so inherently powerful, others can recall and retell it. Story also has the ability to help the listener embrace how they may need to change, because the message transfers into their heart and mind.

FACTS AREN'T AS MEMORABLE AS STORIES

COLD, FACTUAL, OBJECTIVE.

5%

Only 5% remembered
individual statistics.

VS.

WARM, EMOTIONAL, SUBJECTIVE.

63%

Yet 63% remembered
the stories.

Communicate Data to Lead

There's nonstop buzz about data, big data, small data, deep data, thick data, and machines that are learning to analyze data. Many organizations are doing cool things that are supposed to improve our lives because of, you guessed it, data. Of course, not all answers to organizational problems or opportunities will pop out of an algorithm.

Data is limited to recording the past by cataloging numerical artifacts of what has happened. Seeking historical truth is vital to good decision-making, and those who work with data are, by nature, truth-seekers. Yet, as you grow into leadership positions, you'll spend most of your time communicating about the future state others need to create with you. **Communicating data shapes our future truth—our future facts.** Communicating it well is central to shaping a future in which humanity and organizations flourish.

Insights from the past inform the direction we need to go and the actions we need to take, but getting others to move forward with these actions only happens when someone communicates well.

The foundation of effective communication is empathy. Ensuring that others understand what you are proposing must trump any personal or professional preferences you have regarding data. A chart that is clear to you could be perplexing to many others. It's not that your audience isn't smart; it's that they are coming from a different background, and often have a different depth of knowledge about data analysis than you do. What you may think is oversimplifying will be perceived by others as blessedly clear.

This book is about communicating data, and that requires tailoring your message to those receiving it. Most data insights reveal the need for a recommendation (also known as a proposal, action plan, or report.) Sometimes, approval for the action you're recommending comes from the executive suite. The best communicators make data concise and clearly structured while telling a convincing and memorable story.

Creating visual and verbal clarity directs attention to key findings so others don't have to work hard to understand why your recommendation should be approved. Mastering the skill of efficient and inspiring communication pays great dividends.

Communicating data effectively isn't about creating sexy charts and showcasing your smarts. No, it is about knowing the right amount of information to share, in what way, and to whom.

**CAREER PROGRESSION BY INVESTING
IN COMMUNICATIONS SKILLS**

INSPIRE

LEADER

Inspire action in others by
delivering a presentation
that makes data stick.

EXPLAIN

STRATEGIC ADVISOR

Explain your point of view
through story-structured
recommendations in a Slidedoc™.

EXPLORE

INDIVIDUAL CONTRIBUTOR

Explore and analyze data
for others to interpret.

Invest Time in Communication Skills

While the number of jobs that utilize data is increasing rapidly across all industries, a command of data science isn't the skill most desired by employers. Strong communication is.

In late 2018, Jeff Weiner, CEO of LinkedIn, shared findings of a study the company conducted on skills gaps in the work force. Using their Talent Insights tool, job openings posted online were compared to the skill sets of candidates available to fill them. The number one skills gap was soft skills. **Out of a soft skills gap of a whopping 1.6 million, 993,000 required oral communication skills, and 140,000 required writing skills.** Weiner concluded that people with strong communication skills will not be replaced by emerging technology such as artificial intelligence.

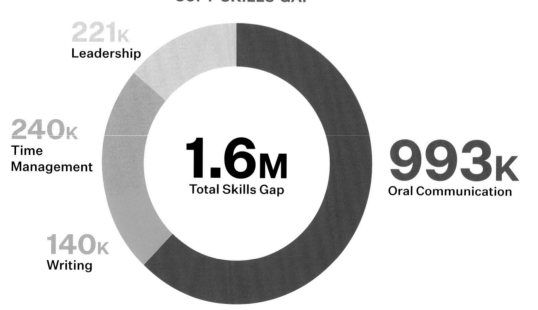

SOFT SKILLS GAP

221K
Leadership

240K
Time Management

140K
Writing

1.6M
Total Skills Gap

993K
Oral Communication

Another body of research conducted by Burning Glass Technology for IBM found that employers require data scientists to be more proficient in soft skills than almost all other jobs.[6] They want employees who can couple data exploration with strong problem-solving and writing skills.

Notice that creativity is on the list, too. Granted, this does not mean they are looking for folks to get creative with numbers. Instead, they're looking for those who are inventive problem-solvers who can use their gut to formulate a point of view about data and invent alternate futures based upon data discoveries.

These soft skills are rarely developed through coursework in science, finance, or statistics; they're cultivated in the liberal arts disciplines. We can't all go back to school to learn them, but the good news is that the methods of communication addressed in this book help close the skills gap.

PERCENTAGE OF DATA SCIENCE JOBS REQUESTING KEY SOFT SKILLS VS. PERCENTAGE OF ALL JOBS

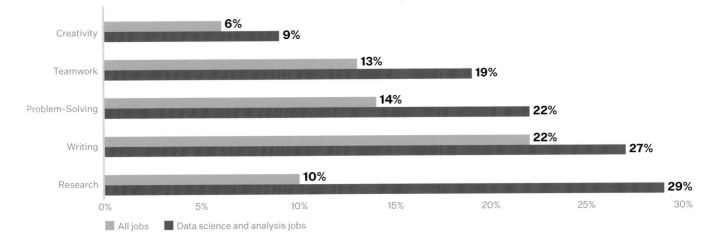

Source: Matt Sigelman, "By the numbers: The job market for data science and analytics," Burning Glass Technologies, February 10, 2017.

Embrace the Power of Story

When you've completed this book, you'll be able to craft a recommendation and inspire action from data using storytelling techniques. Leaders in all sectors spend large sums of money collecting and analyzing data, yet the value comes when someone convincingly communicates what data reveals.

For this research, I pulled thousands of data slides from our clients at Duarte, Inc. Why use slides instead of plotted charts? The brightest strategic thinking and smartest visual and verbal communication in organizations are usually delivered in the form of slide decks. We took a cross-section of data slides of the highest-performing brands in the world from a wide range of sectors, including the consulting, consumer, technology, financial, and healthcare industries. My team classified the chart types, and, most importantly, the words used in relation to data.

Many slides were from Slidedocs™, which are decks of slides with dense words and pictures that are circulated to be read instead of used as formal presentations.

This book doesn't have many charts, and those included are much simpler than ones you may use. I found that complex charts tempted readers to focus on the minutiae of examining the data, which is not the topic of this book. This book is about how data is communicated, not formulated. You will notice the data sets are simple.

The charts are as industry-neutral as possible to keep the most salient insights front and center.

As a student of storytelling, I've come to have great respect for language, including grammar, so I want to acknowledge that the singular form of "datum" isn't common in today's parlance. So, in instances when treating data in the plural sounded goofy, I used the singular instead.

Ah, communication; it can be hard. But the payoffs are extraordinary. If you put the work into developing communication skills, you'll see your career and company do things you never thought imaginable.

Please enjoy,

nancy

"Oh, the stories data would tell, if there were a teller to tell them well."

NANCY DUARTE

COMMUNICATE
DATA TO OTHERS

CHAPTERS

I.

Becoming a
Communicator of Data

II.

Communicating
to Decision-Makers

Becoming a Communicator of Data

Invest in Data Communication Skills

Virtually every company in every industry already has access to vast stores of intelligent data that can offer a competitive advantage. International Data Corporation forecasts a tenfold rise in worldwide data by the year 2025.[7] That's somewhere in the realm of 175 zettabytes.*

Digital tools passively listen to and watch us constantly, monitoring our every move. We can use data to invent new business models, help employees become more productive, and improve customer experiences. Customers now expect the data they want to use to be easily accessible at any time, wherever they are in the world. If you don't provide that, your organization could lose.

The challenge of collecting, storing, analyzing, and providing all of that data is daunting, and yet the bigger challenge is using the data well to drive decisions. To make sense of the overwhelming onslaught, more people in a greater number of roles must understand how to leverage the various kinds of data at their disposal and bring the findings to life. **Executives must constantly make decisions based largely upon data analysis. They want it presented to them in an expert manner.**

Marketing has market analytics, sales has conversion rates, software developers have code churn, HR measures retention, and academics, scientists, policy specialists, and engineers must pull insights out of complex data as a foundation of their work. According to PwC, 67 percent of job openings are for roles that are analytics-enabled.[8] I expect you've come to this book because you're in some such job.

Maybe you have a job that requires you to live in data all the time and dig discoveries out of it, or maybe you regularly have to leverage data as a secondary part of your job, whether in your own decision-making or reporting to others. Perhaps you often give presentations that are based significantly on data, which might be findings of your own or those of others. Or maybe you're just getting started learning how to incorporate data into reports or presentations.

No matter what your role, your career trajectory will get a big lift from knowing how to first understand, then explain, findings in data well. If you learn how to communicate data clearly and persuasively, you will stand out from others.

A zettabyte is a 1 followed by 21 zeros, or 1,000,000,000,000,000,000,000 bytes.

"Today, for anyone who wants a shot at a well-compensated position . . . comfort with data is increasingly essential."[9]

JOSH BERSIN
DELOITTE

Explain Data Through Storytelling

A significant skill threshold stands between exploring, explaining, and inspiring with data. Your career path can stop at analysis, or it can advance into more advanced problem-solving with creative and critical thinking. When this is coupled with the strong skill of communicating well, you'll become a driver of change as your recommendations get approved and deployed.

Move from a heads-down contributor

EXPLORE →

IDENTIFY A PROBLEM OR OPPORTUNITY

For some of you, the exploration of data is very comfortable. Maybe you spend much of your time diving into pools of raw data looking for patterns or potential problems and opportunities, crisscrossing through tables, and pulling nectar of insights from charts. That work can be wonderfully energizing. You can feel like a detective let loose in a *Choose Your Own Adventure* book.

Some data lovers consider it beyond their pay grade to make recommendations about what higher-ups should do with regard to their discoveries. They see themselves as stewards of data, keeping it in good shape and making sure it's accessible. That's just fine if people are okay with their career path ending with data exploration. But if they'd like to move into roles that help determine what an organization should do in light of data findings, they must develop communication skills. As artificial intelligence and machine learning get smarter, only exploration of data will put your role at risk. You must learn how to communicate where data is suggesting the organization should go.

**Move to inspiring
change from data**

EXPLAIN →

RESOLVE THE PROBLEM OR OPPORTUNITY

For others, digging into pools of data to build a case for some course of action is your norm, and you now want to become more adept at influencing others to take action.

Making a recommendation requires that you first judge the data: This chart went up. Was that good? Was it expected? Should we keep going in this direction, or change course? Do we have all the data we need to make a good decision?

Then you've got to construct a point of view based upon your conclusions. Communicating that point of view takes guts. For some of you, it will be crossing a chasm in your career, taking a leap into an exciting but perhaps nerve-wracking position of greater responsibility. Making a recommendation comes with great responsibility, but also accountability. How well you present a case can be a make-or-break, career-defining moment. If you learn to present recommendations well, you will become a trusted advisor.

Become Like the Mentor in a Story

A mentor plays an important role in most stories. At a moment when the hero is stuck, the mentor provides the insight that shows the way—giving others just what they need, in the nick of time, to make them successful on their journey.

Usually, the mentor has a magical gift or tool they've mastered that the hero will need, as when Obi-Wan Kenobi gave Luke a lightsaber and taught him about the Force.

What does this have to do with data? When you use your data to provide timely and critical guidance to decision-makers, you change organizational outcomes. You become the mentor, and your data is the magical tool that gets them unstuck on their journey. Giving others data in the nick of time brings greater success in reaching a desired goal.

There are three ways to use data as a magical tool.

- **Reactive:** Use data after it's collected to sound an alarm so others know there's a problem.

- **Proactive:** Use data to proactively avoid or accelerate something.

- **Predictive:** Identify patterns to anticipate what might happen next.

Those who develop this skill are likely to become highly respected go-to advisors, chosen to participate in higher-profile forms of decision-making.

HAYMITCH + KATNISS	MR. MIYAGI + THE KARATE KID	JIMINY CRICKET + PINOCCHIO	RON SWANSON + LESLIE KNOPE
COACH BOMBAY + THE MIGHTY DUCKS	ASLAN + THE PEVENSIE CHILDREN	MUFASA + SIMBA	MORPHEUS + NEO
THE GOOD WITCH + DOROTHY	ALFRED + BATMAN	Q + BOND	CLARENCE THE ANGEL + GEORGE BAILEY
PROFESSOR DUMBLEDORE + HARRY POTTER	FAIRY GOD- MOTHER + CINDERELLA	MARY POPPINS + MICHAEL AND JANE BANKS	UNCLE BEN + PETER PARKER

Resolve a Spectrum of Problems and Opportunities with Data

Business leaders make thousands of decisions per day, and virtually all of them involve data. Some are quite straightforward, while others are highly complex. Still others involve leaps into the unknown.

Decision-making is the lifeblood of a highly functional organization. Sometimes, you've got to monitor an ongoing stream of multiple dashboards while vigilantly looking for significant changes. Other decisions require pulling together vast amounts of information from inside and outside the company (social and technological trends, for example), and relating it to the organization's business. It is helpful to categorize the range of decisions into three groups: discrete, operational, and strategic.

THREE LEVELS OF DECISIONS MADE FROM DATA

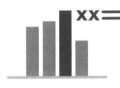

DISCRETE

Discrete decisions may require just one dip into a given dataset. Produce a chart, and you have the answer. One data point can validate stopping or starting something, beginning another, or continuing with what you're doing because it's the right way. Checking your gut against the data can bring clarity to a simple or complex question.

You may decide to renew an ad campaign, see how much sales have dropped with a price increase, or understand variations in profit month-over-month.

OPERATIONAL

Operational decisions involve assessing an ongoing feed of performance data: daily, weekly, monthly, quarterly, and annually.

Real-time dashboards are primarily used for tracking this data, allowing you to make good recommendations by applying a watchful eye and evaluating whether the data are going as expected, or whether there's an unanticipated anomaly that warrants further investigation or changes.

STRATEGIC

Strategic decisions are made by synthesizing information from various sources to determine an organization's future. Some strategic decisions can change the whole course of a business, industry, or the entire world.

These decisions—about whether to buy out a competitor, make a big bet on a new product, enter into a partnership, or launch a new employee benefits program—can be daunting. Accessing the right data, presented effectively, is vital.

Move into a Creative Process

Business moves so fast today that we sometimes have to make decisions without the data we'd like. Even with so much data at hand now, we're not always going to be able to find definitive support for decisions within it.

Overreliance on data to drive decisions can lead to analysis paralysis. When it comes to strategic decisions (and some operational ones, as well), you are anticipating the future, which is, by definition, unknown. Almost all data is historical—a record of what has already happened. It's a recording of what was or what is, not what could be. That means you need to use creative thinking and problem-solving to help shape the future state.

We've all heard the phrase "the data speaks for itself," but the truth is, it almost never communicates clearly for itself. We have to give it a voice. In making decisions about the future, even what you predict to be a clear trend line may not be reliable. Trends can turn incredibly quickly.

To be clear, I'm not talking about getting creative with data or letting bias into your algorithms or conclusions. Creative thinking is used only after you're confident the truth is reflected in your data. Use creativity only for imagining the best actions to take next.

Making good recommendations from data requires a combination of data analysis and intuition, along with a degree of imagination and argumentation. Making a good recommendation involves more than presenting data that proves—or disproves—your hypothesis. That's just a starting point. A recommendation then takes the creative step of proposing which action should be taken, and a good one makes a persuasive case for that action.

This involves taking a big leap from making sense out of data to telling a meaningful story with it. You narrate the story the data has led you to.

If you have been operating in a well-worn mental groove of analytical thinking, you may feel a bit out of your element at first. But stepping out of an analytical mindset and into creative mode is highly energizing and fulfilling. When you see your insights coming alive for people and inspiring them to action, it's deeply satisfying.

TIP ▶ When you need to shift into creative mode, move into a different space than the one in which you crunch your numbers. Signal to your brain to work in a different modality by changing your work area.

TURN DATA INTO ACTION THROUGH CREATIVE THINKING

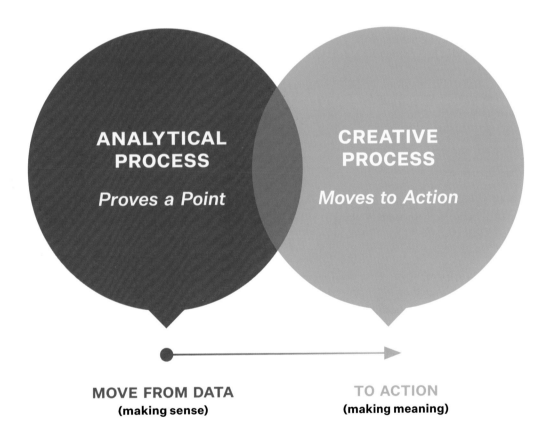

ANALYTICAL PROCESS

Proves a Point

CREATIVE PROCESS

Moves to Action

MOVE FROM DATA
(making sense)

TO ACTION
(making meaning)

Cultivate Your Intuition

Progressing in your career toward management and leadership requires making decisions not only with your head, but also from your gut. Staying in your head and relying too much on data and analysis can lead to stunted and overly safe decisions.

Say your data shows that if you add a second click to cancel a SaaS subscription, fewer clients unsubscribe. The data may also show that adding three or more clicks reduces client churn even more. Your gut tells you that the annoyance this causes clients could lead to long-term damage that's harder to measure. It might also undermine the company's reputation and make winning back lost clients even harder.

Marissa Mayer, former Google executive and Yahoo CEO, now co-founder of Lumi Labs, is renowned for using data to make decisions. She doesn't make choices based solely upon the data collected, however. According to the Masters of Scale podcast, "Each table of data she builds is like a diving board. The higher she builds it, the wider the view, and the bigger the splash when she jumps. But whether she actually takes that dive or not? That's still based on intuition."[10]

" I like to be data-driven, but I don't ignore the human instinct element of it. I roll around in the data, get to know it and understand it really well ...and then make a gut-based call, which is often supported by data and a lot of hard-to-articulate factors, as well." —Marissa Mayer

Sometimes, the best decision to make is a counterintuitive one. Choosing the right direction may not come from data, but may require envisioning a future you are inventing, that data cannot predict. I've had many friends who worked directly for Steve Jobs, and one thing all of them have shared about his decision-making is that no matter how much they prepared, how exhaustively they dug into data, or how many choices they provided him, he always went in an unexpected, counterintuitive direction. He saw ahead to a future impossible to prepare for.

Not so many years ago, leaders had little to no data. Much of their action was based upon gut assessments. In my own business, I've seen how valuable relying on intuition can be. I've made many decisions counter to the data. In the dot-com crash, the economy was in a tailspin, and Silicon Valley took a significant financial hit, which meant my business did, too. Instead of keeping all cylinders running in our four creative services—print, web, multimedia, and presentations—I chose to shutter three of them and focus solely upon presentations. The data didn't say to do that. Yet my gut told me that by being laser-focused on one thing, the firm had the best chance of making it through. I was able to keep our team intact as many other firms closed, and when the economy began to recover, our business spiked at an unprecedented growth rate.

The great mathematician John Tukey said,

"An approximate answer to the right problem is worth a good deal more than an exact answer to an approximate problem."

Those in leadership positions are more generally aware of this because they have to make decisions with limited data to support them all the time. They will be impressed by your gutsy use of intuition as long as you offer a well-formulated recommendation and present it well.

On this note, before we dive in and learn how to shape data into effective communications, the next chapter will take a hard look at who you're communicating with.

"It is not enough to do your best; you must know what to do, and then do your best."

W. EDWARDS DEMING

Communicating to Decision-Makers

Know Your Decision-Maker

When preparing to communicate data, think through who will be involved in its approval, and tailor your approach to appeal to them.

Consider carefully what different audiences need to hear, and how they want to hear it. Whenever your audience changes, so should the language you use. The higher their level of authority, the more structured and brief your approach should be. You should also be prepared for rigorous and intrusive questioning.

This chapter and the rest of the book focus on making recommendations to executive decision-makers. They're the toughest customers, and the ones people are generally the most intent to learn how to appeal to. Once you know the best approaches for persuading them, you can easily draw upon these elements for recommendations you make to anyone.

Your decision-maker might be a shareholder, customer, or even a union representative. The concepts outlined here support how to communicate with them, but I've chosen to use internal decision-making for the basis of this book.

KNOW YOUR AUDIENCE

SPEAK SHORTHAND	PROVE YOUR POINT	GET TO THE POINT

PERSUADE PEERS

Use familiar language

To get your own team or peers on board, you need to speak your geek. You probably already have common goals and a common language. The people closest to you organizationally may already understand why you're making the recommendation, and some of them may have helped you craft it and already be on board. It's okay to use the visual and verbal shorthand your team uses on a day-to-day basis. Acronyms, departmental verbiage, and complex charts are all okay, just as long as they are familiar to all involved.

PERSUADE MANAGERS

Be exhaustive by including an appendix

Managers must be confident that recommendations are well-informed and defensible. If they're going to take action on them, their reputations should not be on the line. They're not going to risk taking a hit for a poorly constructed idea. You need to show that you've done your homework, and present your thinking clearly. Keep your recommendation crisp, but for your boss attach a comprehensive appendix that includes your research and any other supporting evidence. If you do a good job, your boss may even sponsor your idea by having you present it to the executive team.

PERSUADE EXECUTIVES

Write brief, logical, rigorous recommendations

We're all busy, but still it's hard to comprehend just how busy executives are. You must craft a recommendation for them with a tight structure that is brief and easily skimmable. If you are presenting to them and have been given 30 minutes, take 15 so they can ask questions. Be extremely clear, and prepare to be grilled. Also, tailor the way you communicate to a style they prefer. They all have particular preferences. Your approach should match their communication style, not yours.

Respect Their Time; Executives Are Busy

Time is short for everyone, but it is especially so for executives. They have a lot riding on how they spend their time, with many competing demands. They must drive the strategic agenda, stay on top of markets, and ensure that customers, employees, shareholders, and boards are happy.

Executives bear a mental and emotional load of responsibility that would scare most people. And, if time is the most valuable commodity they have, people who communicate with them clearly become valuable. How well others research and construct recommendations can give them back time.

I know a woman who reported directly to the CEO at a public company. She was so trusted, she could text a short, well-structured recommendation to the CEO in the company jet and get a reply with a decision almost immediately.

My friend no longer needed to provide the CEO with backup data, and the CEO no longer questioned the process of getting to the recommendation.

HOW CEOs LEVERAGE TIME

These habits of some famous CEOs indicate how busy they are and how disciplined they must be with their time.

TIM COOK

CEO of Apple; begins each day at 4:30 a.m. to keep up with sending and responding to emails.[11]

INDRA NOOYI

Former CEO of Pepsi; authorized her assistant to give her children permission to do things like go to a friend's house after school.[12]

SHELLYE ARCHAMBEAU

As a board member at Verizon and Nordstrom, she saved three hours a week by cutting off most of her hair so she could spend less time attending to it.[13]

RICHARD BRANSON

The founder of Virgin books time with family in his work calendar.[14]

HOW I LEVERAGE TIME

As a CEO and author, I took comfort in reading about these practices, because I use similar strategies to optimize my time. I'm not sharing the craziest ones here, because I'd like to retain some dignity.

For example, when I'm on a book deadline, I start my day at 5 a.m. and block it to 11 a.m., just for writing. I can't check email, because if I get an urgent or agitating message, my focus is shot for the rest of the morning.

My assistant books my family vacations and parties. We also use a secret code for who should or shouldn't make it onto my calendar. I wash my hair three times a week, and let it air-dry for an hour while I answer emails in the mornings, which cuts down on blow-drying time.

I bring physical printouts in need of signatures or feedback on flights so I can take advantage of the time during takeoff and landing, when electronic devices have to be off. Upon landing, I send them from a travel scanner.

Know How Executives Are Measured

Executives are under incredible pressure to perform. Companies are like elaborate ecosystems, and executives must ensure that disparate moving parts are kept in harmony.

No single job description covers the responsibilities of every executive at all organizations, but performance is almost universally assessed according to the measures below. Executives drive success through six primary levers of performance. If your recommendation involves improvement of results in one of these areas, it will likely have to be approved by an executive.

EXECUTIVE PERFORMANCE LEVERS

Drive up revenue and profit
Financial strength is critical to an organization's ability to pay the bills, compensate staff well, and make financial bets on securing the future.

Drive up market share
They must find ways to gain a competitive advantage to put the company in a dominant market position and identify disruptive trends before competitors do.

Drive up retention
They keep clients, employees, and partners happy to reduce "churn." Retention boosts profit, lowers costs for customers, and strengthens the culture.

EXECS DRIVE UP >   Revenue and Profit   Market Share   Retention

MONEY   **MARKET**   **EXPOSURE**

EXECS DRIVE DOWN >   Costs   Time to Market   Risk

Drive down costs
One of the most effective ways to achieve financial health is to generate strong profit by judiciously identifying cost savings.

Drive down time to market
They work to remove any roadblocks slowing down getting products and services to market first—while still assuring they are fabulous.*

Drive down risk
Reducing operational, legal, compliance, financial, and quality risks mitigates the threat of production stoppage, penalties, and damage to reputation.

A friend of mine told me there are three Fs in getting to market. You're either first, fabulous, or effed. Yup.

All three executive levers are measurable with key performance indicators (KPIs), and almost all KPIs fall into one or more of these areas. If your recommendation is destined for the desk of an executive, it should propose improvement in one of these categories. Addressing these areas will ensure that executives see its value, and they'll be able to tell right away why they have to be involved in approving it.

If you have already formulated a recommendation you are planning to present to an executive, ask yourself right now: does it move one of the executive levers of performance? If that's not clear, dig into how it might, and how you can make a case for that.

HERE ARE A FEW OF DUARTE, INC.'S STRATEGIES FOR THIS YEAR

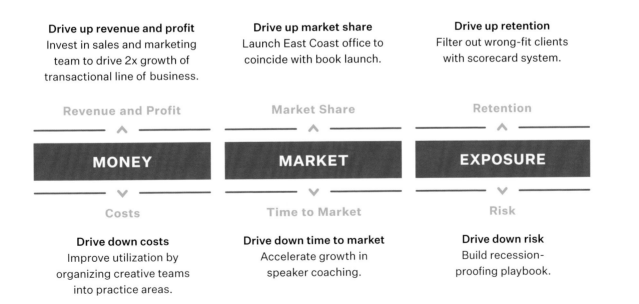

Drive up revenue and profit
Invest in sales and marketing team to drive 2x growth of transactional line of business.

Drive up market share
Launch East Coast office to coincide with book launch.

Drive up retention
Filter out wrong-fit clients with scorecard system.

Revenue and Profit

Market Share

Retention

MONEY

MARKET

EXPOSURE

Costs

Time to Market

Risk

Drive down costs
Improve utilization by organizing creative teams into practice areas.

Drive down time to market
Accelerate growth in speaker coaching.

Drive down risk
Build recession-proofing playbook.

Understand How Executives Consume Information

Executives have personal preferences in how they receive recommendations. To communicate to them, find someone who can mentor you in understanding these preferences. Some executives read every last word of a thick report, or may want brief summaries with the important bits flagged.

You must know everyone involved in the approval process, and you may need to tailor your approach in a number of different ways to appeal to each of them. For example, each person on my executive team has their own communication preferences, and many are different from mine. Some prefer email, others prefer Slidedocs, and still others prefer quick, one-on-one discussions.

Ideally, the person you choose to advise you about preferences knows the executives well. Seek out someone who has spent time with them and has experience communicating with them. This information is useful for all types of communications with executives, such as meetings and email. Your legwork will pay good dividends.

My direct reports know that for electronic communication, I like email—don't even try to message me! The way I process longer, written information is to read it ahead of meetings and make notes about questions I have. Depending on whether an issue is urgent or not, they know to contact my assistant. The best way to get approval from me is with a one-on-one meeting or a quick call.

Styles vary a whole lot. Some executives may make decisions on their cellphones from the corporate jet; others use printouts or write digital notes on a tablet. They may only have time for you to ride along in their car to the airport to review your recommendation. And, if a recommendation has impressed the executive, you may be asked to give a formal presentation to the entire board.

Knowing who you are making a recommendation to and how they like to receive information can make or break not only how a recommendation is received, but how you are viewed for career opportunities, as well.

TIP ▶ Download a one-pager template for recommendations at duarte.com/datastory and see an example on page 211.

KNOW HOW EXECUTIVES PREFER TO COMMUNICATE

Each executive has personal preferences for how they receive and process information.

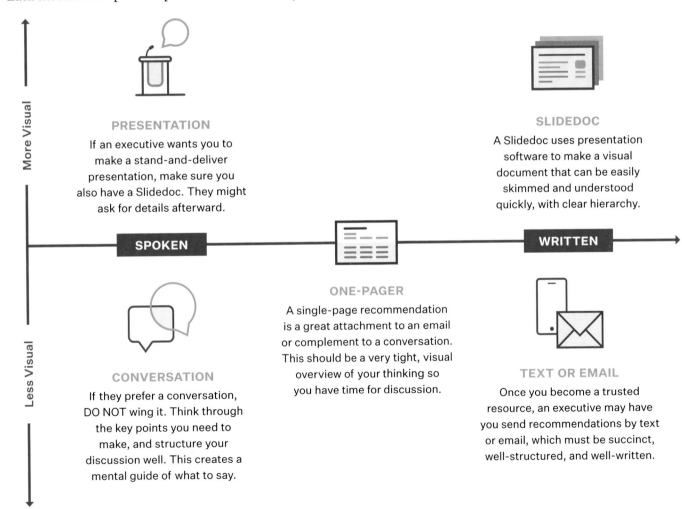

More Visual

PRESENTATION

If an executive wants you to make a stand-and-deliver presentation, make sure you also have a Slidedoc. They might ask for details afterward.

SLIDEDOC

A Slidedoc uses presentation software to make a visual document that can be easily skimmed and understood quickly, with clear hierarchy.

SPOKEN

WRITTEN

ONE-PAGER

A single-page recommendation is a great attachment to an email or complement to a conversation. This should be a very tight, visual overview of your thinking so you have time for discussion.

Less Visual

CONVERSATION

If they prefer a conversation, DO NOT wing it. Think through the key points you need to make, and structure your discussion well. This creates a mental guide of what to say.

TEXT OR EMAIL

Once you become a trusted resource, an executive may have you send recommendations by text or email, which must be succinct, well-structured, and well-written.

Expect Questions and Interruptions

An executive makes many decisions every day. Sometimes, they are made briskly, but other decisions require deeper thought.

When it comes to recommendations, many of my CEO friends spend one full day per month listening to their management teams present recommendations. Their teams propose ideas in 30-minute increments for them to approve, decline, or ask for more information as a key part of their executive function.

If you are asked to present a recommendation to an executive, or perhaps the whole executive team at one of their meetings, you must be prepared to be interrupted before you finish. Way before you finish.

Isn't that rude? No. Most executives are in positions of leadership because they can swiftly assess information and challenge it well. As they begin to get the gist of your recommendation, they immediately start seeing pros and cons. They interrupt you to get answers as fast as they can to key questions prompted by their deep business knowledge. **In an effort to be expedient, they will cut in to gain clarity on the full picture of what you're suggesting, and how well you've thought it through.**

What you prepared so logically...

...will go haywire quickly.

It's as if the moment they hear your fundamental idea, it forms a picture in their minds, but the picture is blurry in parts, or has some gaps, so they ask questions to fill those in.

Often, they'll hop all over the place, pelting you with questions. You need to mentally prepare for the intensity of that. Also, allow time for them to question you. Don't fill up the entire time slot you're given with your presentation. It's important to know how long you have, so if you're not told, ask. Most executive meetings get chopped into half-hour increments, so a good general rule is to formally prepare only 15 minutes so you have time for questions.

You should also ask the person who suggested that you present to the executives about what to expect. Ask about the types of questions you should be prepared for. Take time to anticipate what those might be, but you probably won't be able to put your finger on all of them. Your sponsor may not either, so prepare to be surprised. You don't want to come across as a deer caught in the headlights.

A sponsor will help you understand:

- The strong opinions executives have that might be out of your purview.

- Where they may want to dive deep, and which kinds of information should be provided if they do.

- The counterarguments they might pose, and how you should prepare for them.

While you must rigorously trim down the information you present, you should also conduct extensive research to support your recommendation. Make sure you have a good mental command of it so you can call it to mind quickly under pressure.

The consequences of even one failed decision by an executive could bring unsurmountable internal and external chaos, or even epic public humiliation for themselves and the company.

Let them interrupt you.

"The inability to make decisions is one of the principal reasons executives fail."

JOHN C. MAXWELL

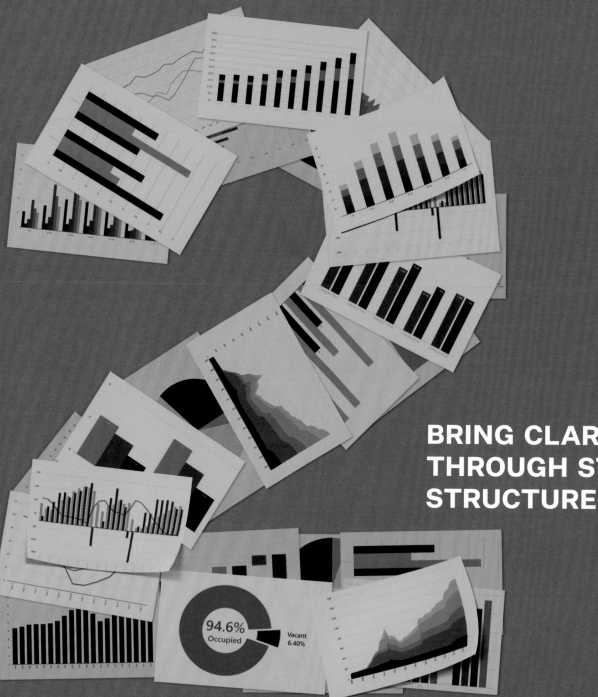

**BRING CLARITY
THROUGH STORY
STRUCTURE**

CHAPTERS

III.

Crafting a Data
Point of View

IV.

Structuring an
Executive Summary
as a DataStory

V.

Creating Action
Through Analytical
Structure

Crafting a Data
Point of View

Formulate Your Data Point of View

As you explore data, you'll begin to formulate thoughts about what it's telling you. A point of view will emerge from your deep thinking. Sometimes, what you've uncovered will be blatantly self-evident to everyone and based 100 percent on the data. Sometimes, you will have to use a pinch of intuition and make some assumptions. Once you've taken a clear stance on what you've found, you're ready to construct a data point of view (DataPOV™).

STRUCTURE THE DataPOV AS A BIG IDEA

Taking a cue from my book *Resonate*, a DataPOV should be structured as a Big Idea. A Big Idea comprises two parts:

YOUR UNIQUE POINT OF VIEW REQUIRES ACTION

Whatever the data is telling you, it's speaking to you. You dove deep into the data to gain perspective. You made nuanced observations, and the understanding you developed about what needs to be done and how to do it is yours. Own it by expressing a point of view and clearly stating the action called for. If no action needs to be taken, there's no reason to make a recommendation.

WHAT IS AT STAKE

You also need to propose what is at stake, whether your recommendation is approved or not. Think through the positive and negative stakes. There is some cost, whether human or financial, to every recommendation. Articulating the stakes clarifies the benefit and risk inherent to a recommendation. Something is always at stake when asking others to take action.

WRITE IT AS A COMPLETE SENTENCE

Your DataPOV is the centerpiece of your entire recommendation, and all other material you present stands in support of it. Make your DataPOV clear by expressing it in a complete, well-constructed sentence. This means you need at least one noun and one verb.

The DataPOV becomes the title page of your recommendation, and you'll use it as the title of your Slidedoc. This way, people will know right away what your recommendation is about, and you'll construct a thoughtful, logical structure to support it.

STRUCTURE A DataPOV AS A BIG IDEA

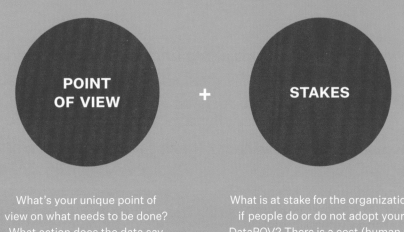

POINT OF VIEW

+

STAKES

What's your unique point of view on what needs to be done? What action does the data say needs to be taken?

What is at stake for the organization if people do or do not adopt your DataPOV? There is a cost (human or financial) to every recommendation.

WRITE THE DataPOV AS A SENTENCE

A sentence contains a noun and a verb. The verb makes it clear what action needs to be taken to change outcomes. The DataPOV succinctly describes the problem or opportunity identified in the data.

Your DataPOV should include the final statistical outcome you desire. This makes it clear what the future will look like if you take the action proposed. Later in the book, you'll discover that your DataPOV will also be the third act (resolution) of your DataStory.

This is a DataPOV

Changing the shopping cart experience and shipping policies could increase sales by 40 percent.

This is not a DataPOV

Fix our online shopping cart.

Understand How Great Brands Communicate with Data

Communicating in verbal or written format requires words. Words are one of the most powerful devices we have to push ideas forward and have them adopted. It makes sense to start by studying patterns in words associated with data.

Finding patterns in data is profoundly satisfying. Much of my work involves pattern-finding. For the book *Resonate*, I analyzed hundreds of great speeches, and found a pattern. For diagrammer.com, I analyzed thousands of diagrams we built for customers, and found a pattern. For this book, I found a number of patterns.

For research, I collected thousands of slides from multiple brands in a cross-section of industries: consumer, hardware, software, social media, search, pharmaceutical, finance, and consultancies. I selected slides randomly from highly-successful public companies and from a wide range of functions and levels, such as sales, marketing, insights groups, analysts, finance, HR, and the executive suite. I used data to determine how to communicate data. How meta.

PATTERNS FOUND IN THE VOCABULARY OF DATA COMMUNICATION

PARTS OF SPEECH

The biggest task was examining the words pulled from data slides. I had a researcher pull the words and then classify them into parts of speech: nouns, adjectives, verbs, adverbs, conjunctions, prepositions, and interjections (we didn't capture pronouns). This led to discoveries about the best ways to use parts of speech, which I have drawn upon throughout the book.

THE IMPORTANCE OF VERBS

I found a fascinating difference in the types of verbs used to present data and those used in non-data slides. Verbs used with data were largely used to describe performance and process, such as "increase sales to drive revenue," whereas verbs used in other slide types had more emotional appeal, such as expressing inspirational, "we can do it" language aimed more at the heart than the head.

PARTS OF SPEECH

BUILDING BLOCKS FOR COMMUNICATING DATA

The parts of speech are important building blocks for driving action. Below is a summary of how and where they are used with data. These will be unpacked throughout the rest of this book.

PARTS OF SPEECH	APPLIED TO DATA	
Verb	**Actions** Actions to be taken as a result of data.	Write a strong recommendation by choosing the best verb modality and strongest strategic verb.
Conjunction	**Connects two or more ideas** Pushes the narrative forward.	Use *and*, *but*, *so*, and *therefore* to construct an executive summary as a story.
Noun	**What you measure** People, places, things, and ideas.	Make it clear which noun you're measuring and how and when you measured it.
Adjective	**Describes static data** Descriptive, observable attributes of static data.	Write observations of bar and component charts using adjectives.
Adverb	**Describes trend line(s)** Descriptive, observable attributes of data over time.	Write observations of line charts using adverbs. A trend line is a verb, so describe it with adverbs.
Interjection	**Marvel at your data** Make an exclamation or sound.	Exclaim how you feel about the data when verbally presenting. *Wow! Isn't it beautiful?*

Choose the Most Effective Action for Your DataPOV

The quality of words chosen can have a large impact on how your idea is received and acted upon. The action to be taken from data is the cornerstone of your DataPOV.

Choosing the best verbs for expressing your DataPOV will make it clear exactly which action you're recommending.

Over 20 years ago, my husband and I hired a life coach to help us construct a life mission statement. The coach told us that the most important part of the statement would be the verb, because the verb specified the actions we were committing to rather than just intentions. The verb would set the terms of how we calendared our time, helping to ensure that we did the activities that would fulfill us most. Since then, I've been a keen observer of verbs, and in the rest of this chapter, I will share patterns from verbs used with data to help refine your DataPOV.

The verbs associated with data have three distinct modalities:

- Change—We need to change who we are or what we are doing.

- Continue—We need to keep going in the same direction.

- Finish—We need to complete this.

As you formulate your DataPOV, identify which verbs solve the problem or exploit the opportunity most effectively.

BE INTENTIONAL ABOUT WHAT YOUR VERB IS ASKING OTHERS TO DO

In stating your DataPOV, it should be clear which of the three action modalities to use. Be specific about the type of change, continuance, or completion you are recommending. Choose verbs from pages 57–58, which are clear and strong enough to push your recommendation forward.

VERB MODALITIES

CHANGE	CONTINUE	FINISH
We need to change who we are or what we're doing.	**We need to keep going in the same direction.**	**We need to complete this, even if that means conceding failure.**
Choose a 'change' verb if your recommendation is about transformation. It could be a big change or a small change.	Choose a 'continue' verb if your recommendation is about endurance. These verbs are in no way a cop-out. Sometimes, full speed ahead is a great course of action.	Choose a 'finish' verb if your recommendation is about completion. Sometimes, completion is about accomplishing a goal, and at other times, it is about calling it quits. It can take as much work to stop things as it can to launch them.

Decipher Performance and Process Verbs

Some recommendations will lead to small actions your team can do, and others become corporate-wide initiatives that could make or break the organization.

Keep in mind that the actions you choose represent a cost to the organization—in money or labor—to get the recommendation done.

CHOOSE THE STRONGEST VERB POSSIBLE

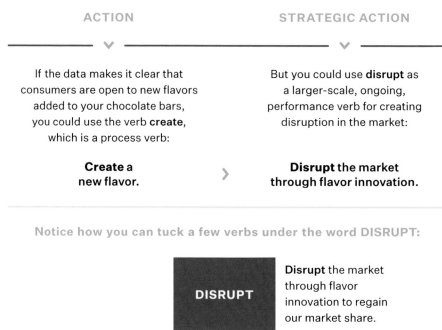

ACTION

STRATEGIC ACTION

If the data makes it clear that consumers are open to new flavors added to your chocolate bars, you could use the verb **create**, which is a process verb:

Create a new flavor.

But you could use **disrupt** as a larger-scale, ongoing, performance verb for creating disruption in the market:

Disrupt the market through flavor innovation.

Notice how you can tuck a few verbs under the word DISRUPT:

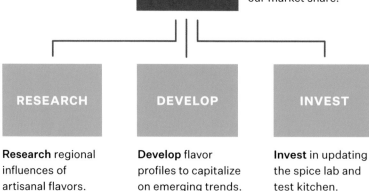

DISRUPT

Disrupt the market through flavor innovation to regain our market share.

RESEARCH

Research regional influences of artisanal flavors.

DEVELOP

Develop flavor profiles to capitalize on emerging trends.

INVEST

Invest in updating the spice lab and test kitchen.

What criteria did we use to categorize words as a process or performance verb? The actions described by performance verbs tend to be measured in numbers over time, through KPIs, whereas the actions described by process verbs tend to be measured as either completed or not. You could say they are binary activities rather than continuous. The data will tell you when you have or have not done them.

Even though the performance verbs tend to be more strategic in nature, both types of verbs can describe strategic activities, depending upon the scale of your recommendation. For example, on the next page, I have classified the verb *build* as a process verb. A DataPOV that proposes a company "build a new plant in Illinois to save $6 million per year" is a very strategic recommendation.

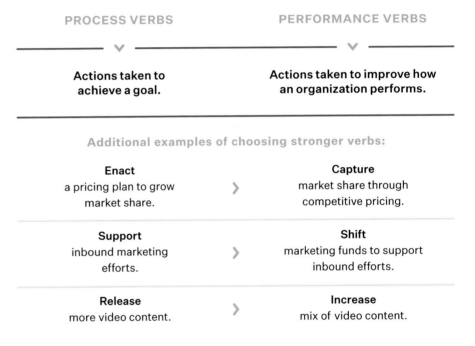

PROCESS VERBS		PERFORMANCE VERBS
Actions taken to achieve a goal.		Actions taken to improve how an organization performs.

Additional examples of choosing stronger verbs:

Enact a pricing plan to grow market share.	>	**Capture** market share through competitive pricing.
Support inbound marketing efforts.	>	**Shift** marketing funds to support inbound efforts.
Release more video content.	>	**Increase** mix of video content.

If an executive is approving your recommendation, if at all possible, use a performance verb. By its nature, the action you're advocating falls into the realm of the levers executives care about (pages 37–38). Remember, executives have their heads squarely in a strategic place most of the time.

Craft Actions with the Best Strategic Insight

The lists of verbs below are grouped according to the three modalities. Tucked beneath them are the performance and process verbs for each. While this list is not exhaustive, these were the most-used verbs in the decks we examined.

CHANGE*

We need to change who we are or what we're doing.

PERFORMANCE VERBS

Accelerate	Decrease	Lessen
Acquire	Deliver	Maximize
Add	Design	Minimize
Advance	Disrupt	Outperform
Allocate	Divest	Prevent
Balance	Enlarge	Recover
Block	Enter	Reduce
Buy	Exceed	Restore
Capture	Expand	Save
Centralize	Extend	Scale
Compete	Gain	Shift
Compress	Grow	Spend
Consume	Impact	Stabilize
Control	Improve	Train
Convert	Increase	
Decentralize	Invest	

PROCESS VERBS

Accept	Divide	Market
Address	Empower	Measure
Adopt	Enable	Migrate
Agree	Enact	Operationalize
Assess	Estimate	Optimize
Assign	Evaluate	Penetrate
Assist	Evolve	Position
Benchmark	Exploit	Produce
Build	Find	Progress
Challenge	Focus	Propose
Communicate	Follow	Recreate
Comply	Gather	Redirect
Concentrate	Generate	Release
Conduct	Get	Renew
Connect	Guide	Repeat
Consider	Help	Require
Converge	Identify	Resist
Create	Ignore	Respond
Define	Implement	Reveal
Delay	Inform	Strategize
Deny	Innovate	Streamline
Develop	Integrate	Structure
Direct	Invent	Support
Discourage	Learn	
Distribute	Leverage	
Divert	Make	

---

*You can add the prefix **re-** to many of the change verbs.*

CONTINUE

We need to keep going in the same direction.

PERFORMANCE VERBS	PROCESS VERBS
Continue	Endure
	Hold onto
	Keep
	Maintain
	Persevere
	Preserve
	Proceed
	Prolong
	Protect
	Remain
	Retain
	Stay
	Survive
	Sustain
	Tolerate
	Uphold
	Withstand

FINISH

We need to complete this, even if that means conceding failure.

PERFORMANCE VERBS	PROCESS VERBS
Arrive	Abandon
Avoid	Attain
Beat	Block
Cancel	Conclude
Cease	Complete
Destroy	Defeat
Discontinue	Dismantle
Eliminate	Drop
End	Obtain
Exit	Reach
Halt	Resolve
Leave	Retreat
Release	Settle
Sell	Sign
Stop	Solve
Win	Surrender
	Withdraw

That's a lot of verbiage about verbs. Nailing down the action with specificity makes it very clear what others will need to do.

"Action is the foundational key to all success."

PABLO PICASSO

Structuring an Executive Summary as a DataStory

Leverage the Structure of a Story Arc

If the brain lights up when a story is told, imagine the power of using elements of storytelling to help your audience understand your DataPOV.

One powerful attribute of stories is how they are structured. Great stories share a framework. Whether it's a personal story told over dinner or one from classical literature or a movie, stories told well usually have a similar three-act structure.

When someone talks about the dramatic arc of a story, they're referring to the three-act structure and how tension rises and falls during the narrative. If the chart to the right had a *y*-axis, it would be labeled *tension*.

DRAMATIC STRUCTURE OF A STORY

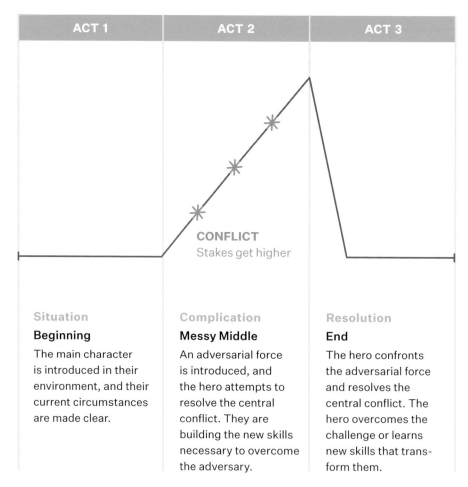

ACT 1	ACT 2	ACT 3

CONFLICT
Stakes get higher

Situation
Beginning
The main character is introduced in their environment, and their current circumstances are made clear.

Complication
Messy Middle
An adversarial force is introduced, and the hero attempts to resolve the central conflict. They are building the new skills necessary to overcome the adversary.

Resolution
End
The hero confronts the adversarial force and resolves the central conflict. The hero overcomes the challenge or learns new skills that transform them.

You can see from the story of Pinocchio *(right),* how the middle is hard. Many call this the messy middle. **There's a lot of conflict during the second act, and the hero has to muster the resolve to overcome it.** Pinocchio works through multiple types of conflict, roadblocks, and temptations. In the end, Pinocchio gets his wish of becoming a real boy. The tension is resolved.

This highly structured three-act framework existed all the way back in Aristotle's Poetics. It organizes content according to the way our brains process information best. Let's see how to apply its power to communicating data through a DataStory.

STORY STRUCTURE OF *PINOCCHIO* (THE 1940 FILM)

ACT 1	ACT 2	ACT 3
A toymaker creates Pinocchio, a wooden puppet, and wishes on a star that he could be a real, live boy.	Pinocchio does come to life, but he is wooden, and must prove himself worthy of becoming a real boy. He's gullible, and crooks lure him to take part in a traveling show. He gets locked in a cage and tells lies, which makes his nose grow. He is tempted to be naughty at Pleasure Island, and he partially transforms into a donkey.	Pinocchio returns home, but his father has been swallowed by a whale while looking for Pinocchio. Pinocchio helps his dad get free from the whale, but dies in the process. Because of Pinocchio's selfless sacrifice, he is worthy of being brought back to life as a real boy.
Situation **Beginning**	Complication **Messy Middle**	Resolution **End**
	⏶ Pinocchio works through a lot of conflict until he reverses his fortune.	

Write an Executive Summary in Three Acts

One of the most important pages in your recommendation is the executive summary, because it is your first interaction with your readers. Their decision to continue reading depends upon their impression of your executive summary.

The rise and fall in a story arc can be applied to the way you structure an executive summary. We call this construction the DataStory. Borrowing from the structure of storytelling makes an executive summary engaging and memorable, and it actually reads much like a story.

Notice how the third act is your DataPOV. It states how you'd like the DataStory to end.

THE THREE ACTS OF A DATASTORY

A DataStory is a concise overview of your recommendation, structured into three acts. Below is a very short executive summary written as a DataStory.

ACT 1	ACT 2	ACT 3
Beginning There is a problem or opportunity identified in the data.	**Middle** It's messy to proceed because the data presents problems and/or opportunities.	**End** The DataPOV addresses the problem at its root, creating a solution with positive outcomes.

The DataStory structure ▶ to the right follows the three-act structure.

Situation	Complication	Resolution
The average subscription renewal rate per region is 62 percent.	**but** Only 23 percent of clients in the western region renew their subscriptions.	**so** We need to tailor our content to appeal to regional preferences to gain market share in the west.

Act 1

The beginning of a DataStory makes the current situation clear. The data uncovers a problem to solve or an opportunity to pursue.

Act One introduces the situation in which your organization currently finds itself.

EXAMPLES OF A DATASTORY

	ACT 1	ACT 2	ACT 3
OPPORTUNITY IN THE DATA	**Situation** Our two-year pilot of onsite college campus recruiting for software developers was well-attended.	**and** **Complication** Entry-level candidates are 28 percent more likely to accept an offer if they meet us at a college fair.	**so** **Resolution** It's time to extend our campus program to five more universities to increase our acceptance rate.
PROBLEM IN THE DATA	**Situation** The contract for our client in Germany stipulates that we cover travel costs, so consultants can't bill for travel time.	**and** **Complication** International travel costs rose three percent last quarter, and our profits for this client are down to two percent.	**so** **Resolution** We need to negotiate our contract to include travel expenses and travel time to lower our costs.

Change the Fortune of the Messy Middle

The middle of a story is full of conflict and complications. This tension makes it engaging, stimulating our brains to root for resolution.

Think about Frodo. He has the treachery of Orcs, Gollum, a poisonous spider, impassible landscapes, and, of course, Sauron himself. And that's only part of it! The audience is rooting for him, comparing themselves to him, learning from him, inspired by him, and relieved that it all works out in the end.

To draw a parallel, organizations are messy, too! They're hotbeds of flawed processes, oppressive regulations, greedy shareholders, unhappy customers, broken systems, and aggressive competitors who seek their demise. Keeping any type of organization performing at a healthy level is hard work, and data can reveal something messy that needs to change. Alternatively, it can reveal an opportunity that will be hard and messy to accomplish. Either way, the middle is m-e-s-s-y.

Act Two of an executive summary contains the data points that need to change. What's the measurement that will be reversed if your recommendation is approved? Or, what are the numbers that will increase with the new opportunity? That is where the "mess" is. Reversing a number or hitting the gas pedal on a number creates a lot of work, because it requires someone to take action. **The numbers in the middle of your story will change direction when the right actions are taken.**

WAYS THE DATA IN THE SECOND ACT MAY NEED TO CHANGE

- Reverse the data
- Continue the data
- Increase the data
- Reduce the data
- Speed up the data
- Slow down the data

Human behavior drives the performance of most business data. It's usually humans who make a statistic go up or down based upon their actions. Their output might be too low, click-through too low, salaries high, satisfaction high, turnover low, heart rate high, inventory late, routing slow, due dates missed, orders damaged, sales down, scrap high, volume flat, and/or emissions high. **All of this data can be turned around by humans taking the right actions.**

Act 2

The middle of the DataStory reveals the central conflict. The data reveals measurable symptoms that must change in some way.

The actions of others will help this data head in the desired direction.

EXAMPLES OF DATASTORY

	ACT 1	ACT 2	ACT 3
OPPORTUNITY IN THE DATA	**Situation** Our new webinar about cloud services attracted more attendees than our historical high.	**and** **Complication** 642 highly-qualified leads came in from the webinar and surpassed all other marketing channels by 22 percent last month.	**so** **Resolution** We should redirect marketing funds to cover quarterly webinars to increase highly-qualified lead flow.
PROBLEM IN THE DATA	**Situation** Our average days for receivables have increased by 10 since June.	**and** **Complication** 50 of our customers are not in compliance with our 30-day payment terms.	**so** **Resolution** If we enforce late-payment fees in our terms, it will create stronger cash flow.

Use Your DataPOV as the Third Act

Everyone loves stories in which the protagonist slays the enemy, falls in love, finds the golden goblet, and is honored as a hero at the end. Yay! Getting there was hard, but the end is so satisfying.

If the second act is a messy statistic that needs to change, the third act describes how the story would end if people took action to change it.

Turn back and review all the third acts in the DataStory examples: page 66, page 68, and page 70. The third act in the executive summary is your DataPOV of how the drama will resolve if people take your proposed action. The verb drives the means by which the organization, customers, employees, and/or others can achieve a more advantageous result.

Not all DataPOVs create what is perceived as a happy ending. Sometimes, you have to choose a verb that requires something to be stopped. Let's say your DataPOV is to "obsolesce a product that's losing money." What might be a happy ending for the company, could create heartbreak for employees or customers who love the product. So, a decision that is positive for the organization may come with some sorrow for others, and must be framed carefully when discussed more broadly (pages 193–194).

Getting others to take action isn't easy.* Executives know this. **Before an executive approves your recommendation, they are weighing the risk versus the reward of your proposal.** They ask themselves: *Is the battle to change this messy data point going to be worth the prize at the end? Will this put us at risk? Will it bring results as quickly as we need?*

An organization's ultimate goal is stronger outcomes, but they must be pursued with awareness of the strain and conflict that may be involved.

After you've put a lot of thoughtful preparation into a recommendation, it could be killed, stalled, or adopted. It depends on how much executives believe the problem or opportunity in the messy middle is a priority, and whether your DataPOV will deliver the desired results.

TIP ▶ You may have noticed the conjunctions *but*, *and*, or *so*. Conjunctions join phrases together and push the narrative along in an executive summary. See Appendix for alternate conjunction choices.

To learn how to communicate through change, check out the book Illuminate by Nancy Duarte and Patti Sanchez.

Act 3

The end of the DataStory is your point of view for how to solve the messy middle and create a positive outcome in the future.

The actions proposed will transform your future data.

EXAMPLES OF DATASTORY

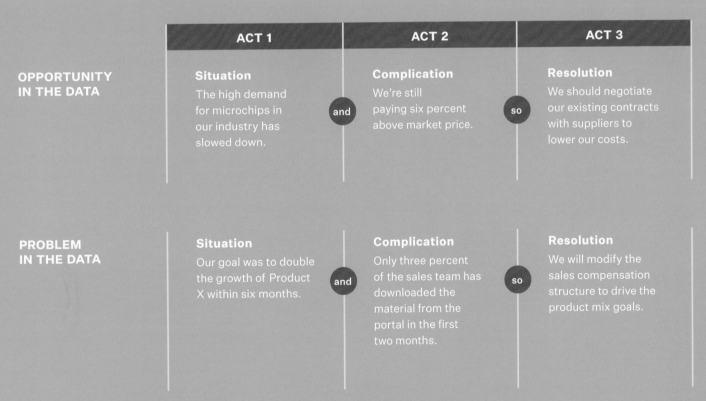

	ACT 1	ACT 2	ACT 3
OPPORTUNITY IN THE DATA	**Situation** The high demand for microchips in our industry has slowed down.	**Complication** We're still paying six percent above market price.	**Resolution** We should negotiate our existing contracts with suppliers to lower our costs.
PROBLEM IN THE DATA	**Situation** Our goal was to double the growth of Product X within six months.	**Complication** Only three percent of the sales team has downloaded the material from the portal in the first two months.	**Resolution** We will modify the sales compensation structure to drive the product mix goals.

(and ... so)

"Tell me the facts, and I'll learn. Tell me the truth, and I'll believe. But tell me a story, and it will live in my heart forever."

NATIVE AMERICAN PROVERB

Creating Action Through Analytical Structure

Blend Logical and Persuasive Writing

Proposing a recommendation that combines the familiar structure of story with the strength and credibility of logic will clarify the decision you are trying to derive from the data.

Crafting a recommendation for approval is a blend of argumentative and persuasive writing. Why? You are not just trying to prove you have your facts right (argumentation). You are also trying to move others to action (persuasion).

A written recommendation from data blends a bit from both types of appeals. Below is a summary of the distinctions between argument and persuasion, which might seem oversimplified to professional logicians, but applied to business, it works.

A RECOMMENDATION BLENDS BOTH TYPES OF APPEALS

	ARGUMENTATIVE WRITING (Logical Appeal)	PERSUASIVE WRITING (Emotional Appeal)	WRITING A RECOMMENDATION (Blend of Both)
Purpose	Construct compelling evidence that your viewpoint is backed by the truth and is factual.	Persuade the audience to agree with your perspective and take action on your viewpoint.	*Use the data available, plus intuition, to form a point of view that requires action from your organization.*
Approach	Deliver information from both sides of the issue by choosing one side as valid and causing others to doubt the counterclaim.	Deliver information and opinions on only one side of the issue, and develop a strong connection with a target audience.	*Develop a DataStory supported by evidence, and also include any counterarguments your audience may have, so they feel you have considered their perspective.*
Appeals	Use logical appeals to support claims with solid examples, expert opinions, data, and facts. The goal is to be right, not necessarily to take action.	Use emotional appeals to convince others of your opinion and feelings, so the audience will move forward on your perspective.	*Structure the appeal as a story; support your recommendation with data and solid evidence that sticks by adding meaning (Section Four).*
Tone	Professional, tactful, logical.	Personal, passionate, emotional.	*Appropriate tone based upon the audience.*

You cannot submit a recommendation to an executive (or anyone, for that matter) if it doesn't have an intuitively logical structure. Without clear logic, your recommendation will take time for others to make sense of, and you will undermine your case. If people don't clearly understand your recommendation and the points that support it, you haven't put enough time into the organization of the information.

In school, you may have learned how to form a solid structure for outlining an essay or winning a debate. That's a bit of what you're doing here. Your structure itself communicates a message about what's important, and in what order. Crafting a good structure helps others see the logic in your thinking, and the process actually strengthens your own thought process. The most widely used structuring devices are an outline or a tree structure.

Notice in the tree structure to the right that all supporting information hangs off the single topic at the top. **In a Recommendation Tree, that unifying point is your DataPOV. All the points below cascade from it. Using a tree structure helps you look at the whole without getting lost in the parts.** This format also helps filter out any tangential subtopics that don't directly support your DataPOV.

HIERARCHICAL ORGANIZATION STRUCTURES

RECOMMENDATION OUTLINE

I. _____
   A. _ _ _ _ _ _ _
   B. _ _ _ _ _ _ _
   C. _ _ _ _ _ _ _
      1. . . . .
      2. . . . .

II. _____
   A. _ _ _ _ _ _ _
      1. . . . .
      2. . . . .
      3. . . . .
   B. _ _ _ _ _ _ _

RECOMMENDATION TREE

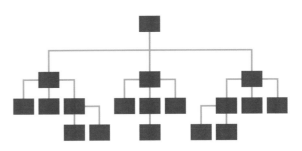

Structure a Recommendation Tree

Slide software is an effective visual communication tool. When you write a recommendation as a Slidedoc, think of each slide as a node within a tree structure.

The cool thing about slides is that the space on a slide is limited, which forces you to be disciplined in streamlining your content. Using one idea per slide helps each point stand on its own while also ensuring that your Slidedoc is logical, yet brief. Each slide should support the DataStory, and you can have as many of them as you see fit. The structure is very flexible.

THE RECOMMENDATION TREE STRUCTURE FOR SLIDEDOCS IS FLEXIBLE

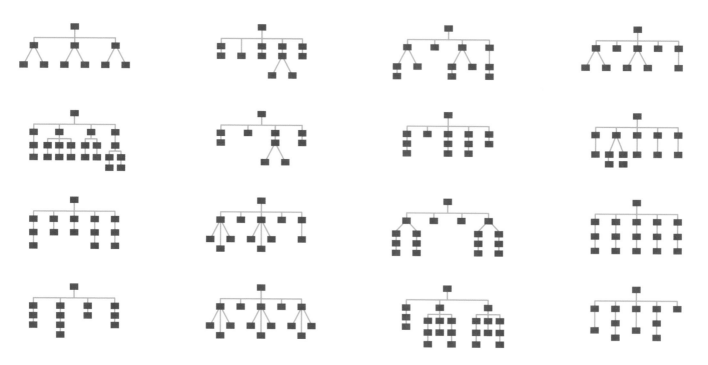

To the right is a Recommendation Tree in which the DataStory is supported by three points (though you can have as many as needed). **I've used a three-prong tree structure throughout the rest of the book for simplicity's sake, and also because when you chunk content together, it becomes more memorable.**[15]

We've been conditioned since we were young to use three supporting points, so you may recognize this. It follows classic, logical argumentation, and even basic essay-writing.

Picture each rectangle as one slide. There is no rigid rule about how many nodes (slides) are needed in the tree. It's as flexible as you need to get your point across, with as much supporting evidence as possible.

TIP ▶ When building a Slidedoc, put the document in Slide Sorter View to ensure that your structure and flow all support the DataStory.

RECOMMENDATION TREE WITH THREE SUPPORTING POINTS

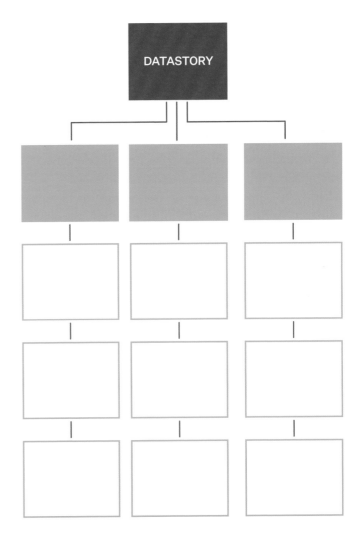

Define Actions to Support Your DataStory

The best way to support the action you are recommending is to break it into smaller actions. When you run (verb), you must swing your arms, pump your legs, and breathe through your lungs. Those are all sub-actions. The way to get traction on your DataStory is to use a series of phrases with verbs to support your main, proposed action.

In the tree to the right in blue, note the conjunction "therefore, we need to..." in the dark, blue rectangle. This is included not because you'd actually put in a slide like that, but as an aid for crafting your action statements. Asking yourself what the actions are that finish the sentence will help push your narrative along by identifying supporting actions. The conjunction begs the question "WHAT do we DO?" and the three sub-actions all answer the question "Therefore, we need to... What? What? What?"

This phrase has become a mantra in my work meetings and conversations. If someone is going on and on about a problem or situation, I'll say, "Therefore, we need to..." and then pause. This is a great way to develop a problem-solving mindset, instead of a problem-identifying one, for ourselves and those we lead.

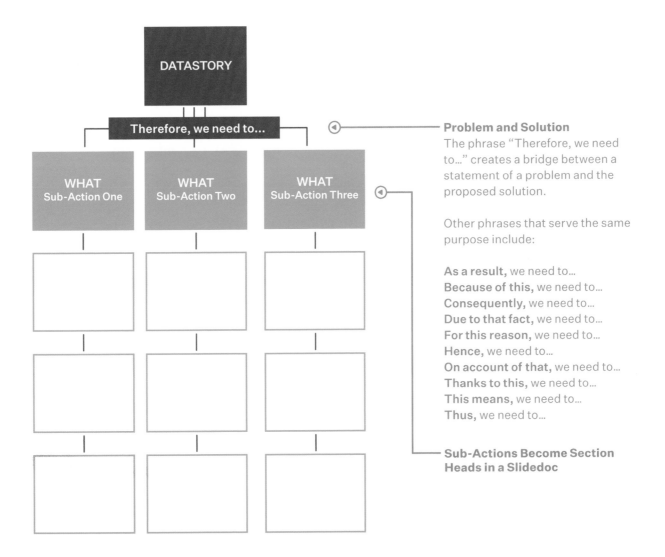

DATASTORY

Therefore, we need to...

WHAT
Sub-Action One

WHAT
Sub-Action Two

WHAT
Sub-Action Three

Problem and Solution
The phrase "Therefore, we need to..." creates a bridge between a statement of a problem and the proposed solution.

Other phrases that serve the same purpose include:

As a result, we need to...
Because of this, we need to...
Consequently, we need to...
Due to that fact, we need to...
For this reason, we need to...
Hence, we need to...
On account of that, we need to...
Thanks to this, we need to...
This means, we need to...
Thus, we need to...

Sub-Actions Become Section Heads in a Slidedoc

Motivate by Explaining Why

When making recommendations, a common mistake is to jump right to a statement of what and how it should be done, skipping WHY altogether.

The people on the receiving end of your recommendation may well be the very ones who have to do the things you recommend. They're going to want you to persuasively tell them WHY the action is necessary. If you explain clearly WHY it's important, your suggestion is more likely to get traction. Keeping in mind who is going to be taking action helps you formulate good supporting points that alleviate the friction stalling or stopping the approval of recommendations.

Be careful, though, not to overdo providing support for WHY. It's tempting to pour every bit of evidence into a Slidedoc, but over-loading with too much information could undermine your perspective.

ANSWERING "WHY" ADDS A PERSUASIVE LAYER

Ask yourself WHY this needs to get done

Keep asking yourself "Why, why, why, why, why?" This is the same process used with root-cause analysis to get to the root of problems or opportunities. Especially when we are using our intuition, the answers to WHY are often hiding in our subconscious, and we have to coax them out.

Some answers to "why questions" come from asking "what questions." **What else is at stake? What data is frightening and should change? What would the state of the human condition be if we did or didn't do this?**

SHARE THE IDEAS YOU ABANDONED AND WHY

Address the various directions your recommendation could have gone

One reason executives interrupt is because they think your recommendation might go in a different direction. Let's say backorders have been piling up, and you've been tasked with finding a way to reduce them. You might consider recommending the purchase of faster production equipment and hiring more production staff, but you've landed on the idea of acquiring a supplier that manufactures the part that has been slowing up production.

An executive may have preferred the option of buying more equipment, and they will want to know you have explored that solution and why you decided against it.

ANSWER WHAT-WHY-HOW TO SUPPORT THE MAIN POINT OF EACH SLIDE

This What-Why-How model brings structure to each slide. You could make actual headlines that ask those questions, or use the model to make sure you've answered them in your prose.

WHAT

WHY

HOW

◀ Asking "What?" will uncover a clear verb, because it answers the question "What needs to get done?"

Asking "Why?" will answer the question "Why do we need to do this, anyway?" It adds a layer of meaning to each slide for the readers.

Asking "How?" will uncover findings about the process, and answers the question "How will we get this done?"

Be Your Own Skeptic

Others may naturally try to find flaws in your point of view. They may view your ideas as truly flawed, or they may just be contentiously kicking up dirt to avoid taking action on the recommendation.

Think about the management above you, your peers beside you, and the direct reports impacted by the recommendation. Think about your customers, shareholders, or employees receiving it.

Think through each group or person who may read your Slidedoc, and anticipate how they might resist. Addressing potential counterarguments may be the most persuasive part of your recommendation. Considering opposing views and counterarguments helps make the recommendation more accurate and defensible.

PLAY THE SKEPTIC

Even if data proves that your position is sound, double-check that you didn't enter the search for evidence with bias.

Play the skeptic and antagonist of your own idea, and cruise through data scenarios that could disprove your claim. Whatever notable objections you think of, include them in your Slidedoc. If you don't thoughtfully present alternative perspectives, your audience is likely to think you failed to consider them.

Ask yourself, "What if the opposite were true?" Also, address any answers that are unknown or unknowable.

CRAFT A COUNTERARGUMENT

Once you've considered all counterarguments, cruise back through the data to cross-check your work. Then, craft a counterargument. State an opposing perspective to your recommendation, and make it very clear that the evidence doesn't support it. Review all the ways your recommendation could be opposed.

After you state a counterargument, oppose it with a transition phrase:

I don't agree…

I completely disagree…

I couldn't go along with that…

I disagree that…

I don't agree with it…

I don't think it…

I have doubts because…

It is difficult to accept because…

There's no way I could agree with that…

This isn't true because…

Include Assumptions by Stating "This Is True If..."

When explaining data, you're also predicting a direction in the future you think the data is telling you to go. This means you are making your recommendation based upon assumptions.

There are two kinds of assumptions: statistical and business. Common statistical assumptions,[16] such as random samples, independence, normality, equal variance, and stability, help to ensure your measurement system is accurate and precise.* These aren't the assumptions I'm concerned with for this book. It's the business assumptions involved in making your recommendation that I'll address.

BUSINESS ASSUMPTIONS TO FORECAST THE FUTURE

No one knows exactly what will happen in the future. You can only make a scientific, wild-ass guess (S.W.A.G.), even with great data. When using data to predict potential outcomes, you are making a case based on conjecture, inference, speculation, and sheer guesswork. Eek. Some of you purists may have just slammed the book shut.

Due to the subjective nature of business assumptions, it's crucial to be transparent about all of those you've made in arriving at your recommendation. A common problem is that most data used in business is outdated the very next day, and a changing dataset may have heavily influenced your conclusions.

For example, in order to forecast your organization's profit over the next five years, you may make assumptions about factors that impact your finances. Your conclusion may be based upon assumptions like interest rates staying constant, donors continuing at current giving rates, or office vacancies remaining high in your area.

Executives are well aware that in order to make predictions with data, we often have to make assumptions like the ones listed above. They'll be impressed that you are up front about them, and that they don't have to ask what they are. Also be prepared to justify them. Otherwise, your recommendation will come into question.

---

*Some industries require you to include all statistical assumptions in a recommendation. Find out if that's the norm in your business. If so, you must include things like when the statistical assumptions were tweaked and what time periods are missing, if data was not deduced or is missing variables, if non-random samples were used, if an axis is not evenly distributed, etc.

EXAMPLES OF BUSINESS ASSUMPTIONS THAT RECOMMENDATIONS MAY BE BUILT ON

If you move forward with a recommendation that depends on assumptions, state them in the form of "This is true if..."

THIS IS TRUE IF...

...revenue continues to grow at 2.5 percent.

...no significant economic fluctuations happen.

...no major technological shifts occur.

...hiring continues at the current speed.

...we have a steady supply of parts and accessories.

...no unexpected competitor appears.

...subscriptions maintain their growth rates.

...the hourly rate stays the same.

...market conditions stay the same.

...pay cuts remain in place.

...no new developments in technology arise.

...survey participants are all low-income.

...we continue to invest in our IT systems.

...we have calculated based upon the current run rate.

*To make a prediction about the future, you must make clear what you assume will remain true, even though there's no concrete evidence to support it. **Business is fluid and changing all the time, and we'd never make decisions if we waited for the data to stand still.** Companies need to make decisions even when there is great uncertainty.*

Review the Components of a Recommendation Tree

We have covered a lot of ground so far, and it seems like the right time to recap by showing the anatomy of a Recommendation Tree. This structure helps guide your thinking so you can construct a Slidedoc in a logical structure to help others make decisions.

To the right is the construction of a Recommendation Tree. Each rectangle represents a potential slide. There's no single way to construct a recommendation because they all vary in complexity, but here is a simple one (annotated).

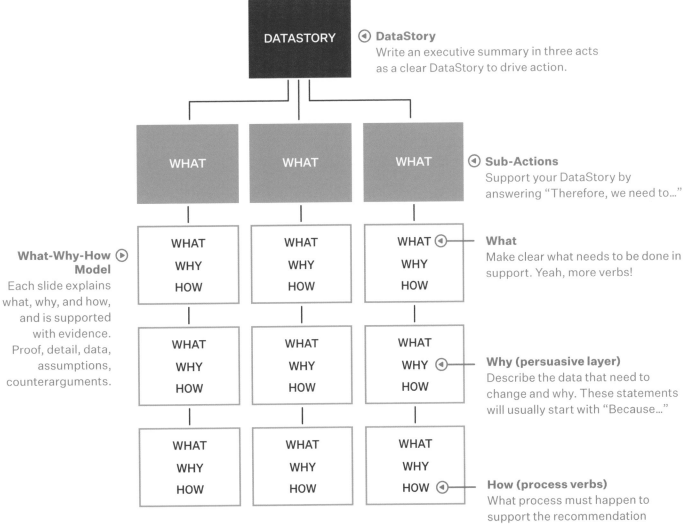

DataStory
Write an executive summary in three acts as a clear DataStory to drive action.

Sub-Actions
Support your DataStory by answering "Therefore, we need to..."

What-Why-How Model
Each slide explains what, why, and how, and is supported with evidence. Proof, detail, data, assumptions, counterarguments.

What
Make clear what needs to be done in support. Yeah, more verbs!

Why (persuasive layer)
Describe the data that need to change and why. These statements will usually start with "Because..."

How (process verbs)
What process must happen to support the recommendation to completion? Make your recommendation clear by explaining HOW things will get done.

"We need a new generation of executives who understand how to manage and lead through data. And we also need a new generation of employees who are able to help us organize and structure our businesses around that data."

MARC BENIOFF
CEO, SALESFORCE

MAKE CLEAR
CHARTS AND
SLIDES

CHAPTERS

VI.

Choosing Charts and
Writing Observations

VII.

Annotating Insights
onto Charts

VIII.

Building a Skimmable
Slidedoc

Choosing Charts and Writing Observations

Choose Charts Everyone Understands

It's important to choose the best type of chart for communicating insights. Many beautiful and engaging ways to plot charts are available today. Huge databases with stunning visual intelligence can display data that whooshes across screens, unveiling clickable layers of data beneath it. As data sets grow ever more vast, charts are getting more complex and sexy.

The use of complex charts and fancy-schmancy business intelligence tools helps uncover insights, but when it comes to explaining the action you are advising, you must share your findings in a visually simple way.

Your audience needs to understand you quickly and clearly, so plot and annotate data in the clearest and most common visual format. **Use charts that everyone is familiar with: bar, pie, and line charts. I know, right? With all the cool new visualization tools, that's what I've got for you?** But remember, this book is in service of getting agreement on action. For gaining buy-in, clarity always outperforms cool.

I'm not saying to disregard all the breathtaking business intelligence tools you may have. Use them to aggregate and explore data. But then articulate your observations in the simplest form that will showcase the key points. This is usually done with a bar, pie, or line chart.

Using charts that are more complex than they need to be adds mental labor to the reviewer and pulls attention away from the key insight.

Complex visualizations can also look so authoritative that they lead people to suspend their judgment and accept the chart as if it is accurate and without bias. This might seem advantageous, but you want others to conclude with insights from the data that are similar to yours. Don't make your conclusions look more certain than they are. Plus, a key insight could be buried in the complexity.

Often, the most profound findings with the greatest impact on an organization are best expressed in remarkably simple graphics. Granted, if you're confident your audience has familiarity with a complex graphic because it's part of the visual language of your industry, then you can absolutely use it.

USE THESE CHARTS TO EXPLORE

Complex charts can be fascinating and look impressive, but they often obscure the main point.

USE THESE CHARTS TO EXPLAIN

Everyone easily processes and understands the bar chart (measures quantity), pie chart (measures parts of 100 percent), and the line chart (measures change over time).

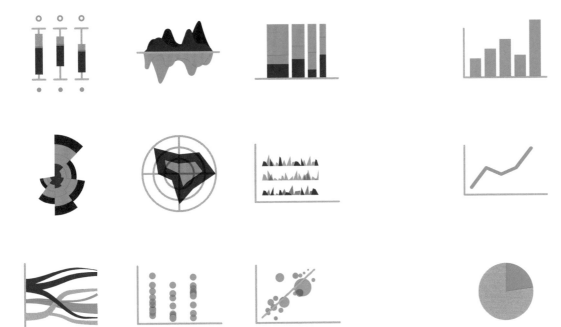

Everyone understands these charts. **Everyone!**

Write Clear Chart Titles

Chart titles are to be factual and neutral. To write one, you need to convey what, how, and when measurement happened. Organizations track concrete nouns (people, places, things) and abstract nouns (ideas) to monitor the health of the organization.

ORGANIZATIONS TRACK NOUNS ALL DAY

NOUNS

Concrete Noun	Abstract Noun
People, places, things	**Ideas, feelings, qualities, states**
Can be seen	Cannot be seen
Data about concrete nouns are counted, measured, and tracked:	Data about abstract nouns are observed, interviewed, and surveyed:

- For **people,** you may measure sick days, headcount, and churn.

- For **places,** you may measure regions or geolocations.

- For **things**, you may measure orders, inventory, and units.

- For **employees,** you may measure engagement.

- For **customers,** you may measure satisfaction.

- For the **market,** you may measure perception.

It's Trickier to Measure Abstract Nouns

Ideas, feelings, qualities, or states are invisible and subjective, which means they cannot always be precisely measured, and may not even be quantifiable at all. Yet some very important things cannot be seen with the eye.

A precise understanding of what you have measured is vital. Are you measuring the quantity of customers, or are you measuring the percentage of online customers who also shop at your retail store? This clarity must be captured in the title of your chart.

Chart Title

Your chart title should be straight-forward, with no fluff; no unnecessary descriptive words allowed. It's simply the noun you measured and when (dates or range of dates). How you measured it (units) is usually on the y-axis.

Example Chart Titles
This chart title is neutral:
2019 Monthly Profit by Percentage

This is not a chart title:
We hit our profit goal this year!

Make Descriptive Observations

If chart titles are factual and neutral, an observation is a statement of insight you have from a chart. An observation supports your perception of the problem or opportunity in the data.

An observation is an additional short statement that frames the chart. It could be placed above the chart title (like the one below), used as a slide title, or inserted as a major subhead within a Slidedoc.

OBSERVATION OF A CHART[17]

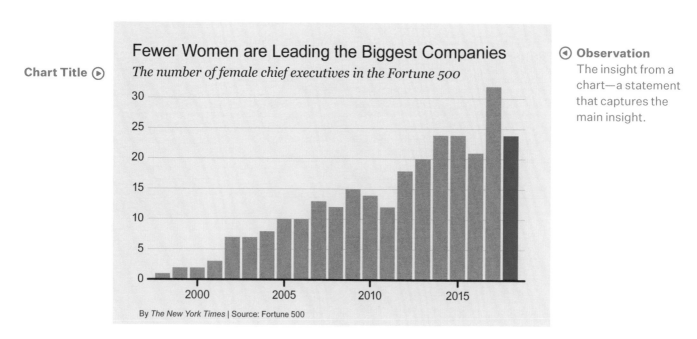

Chart Title ▷

Fewer Women are Leading the Biggest Companies
The number of female chief executives in the Fortune 500

By *The New York Times* | Source: Fortune 500

◁ **Observation**
The insight from a chart—a statement that captures the main insight.

OBSERVATIONS SUPPORT
YOUR CONTEXT

The chart on the left appeared in *The New York Times*. They chose the observation that was important to them, but you could also write the observation as "Female CEOs of public companies spiked in 2017" or "Female CEOs are trending up," and that would also be true. The framing of an observation tells the readers what to focus on.

OBSERVATIONS USE
DESCRIPTIVE LANGUAGE

Two parts of speech may be included in observations:

- **Adjectives are used to describe nouns.**
  In charts, use adjectives to refer to static quantities, such as a yearly total, or a ratio, as in a component chart (pie or waterfall).

- **Adverbs are used to describe verbs.**
  They apply to temporal data, such as trend lines.

If your English is a bit rusty, here's how it works...

Use Adjectives for Bar Charts to Observe Size

Bar charts usually display quantities of nouns. You are observing differences in the height or length of the bars as you compare how similar or different the quantities are in relation to each other. You are observing differences in the size of the bars.

Use the adjectives on the right to help craft an observation about size differences.

BAR CHARTS CONVEY

Most	Least
Grew	Shrank
Largest	Smallest
Higher	Lower
Ahead	Behind
Longer	Shorter
Stronger	Weaker
Leading	Trailing
Greater	Fewer
Better than	Worse than
Greater than	Less than
More than	Less than

RANKED BAR CHARTS CONVEY

More	Less
First	Last
Upward	Downward
Precedes	Follows
Maximum	Minimum
Rising	Falling

**SPLIT AND FLOATING
BAR CHARTS CONVEY**

Wider ——— Narrower

Starts ——— Stops

Begins ——— Completes

To the left ——— To the right

Ahead ——— Behind

Close ——— Distant

Balanced ——— Imbalanced

Lopsided ——— Symmetrical

TIP ▶ You can also use physical attributes to describe the shape produced by the data: saying it looks like a ski jump, that it's tumbling down a hill, or that it's breathing in and then exhaling in a sigh of relief.

Use Adjectives for Component Charts to Observe Ratios

The purpose of a pie or waterfall chart is to give a quick visual snapshot of the part of the whole that's most significant. Highlighting the most important segment(s) makes it easy for readers to comprehend the differences in their sizes.

PIE CHART

A pie chart is really only meant to offer a visual heuristic of the ratios between segments.

If exact differences in size are important, or the viewers can't perceive actual differences in the number they represent, switch to a bar chart.

WATERFALL CHART

Another way you can display ratios well is by using a waterfall chart.

This is a stacked bar chart in which each segment of a bar is spread apart so the ratios between them are made clear. Waterfall charts can show a static snapshot of data or the percentage of change in data over time.

COMPONENT CHARTS CONVEY

Large proportion —— Small proportion

Large percentage —— Small percentage

As much —————— Not as much

Largest ———————— Smallest

A lot ———————————— A little bit

Main part ————————— Lesser part

Majority ——————— Minority

More than ——————— Less than

Most ————————————— Least

All of ————————————— Part of

Significant ——————— Insignificant

Component charts visualize differences in ratios and visually show the proportions or percentages within a quantity of data.

Use the adjectives to the left to help craft an observation about differences in proportion.

Use Adverbs for Line Charts to Observe Trends

Lines are usually used to show how some quantity has changed over time or stayed the same, as the case may be. Use verbs to articulate movement depicted over time.

LINE CHARTS CONVEY

Climb	Steady/decline
Improve	Stagnate
Increase	Flatten/decrease
Recover	Deteriorate
Rise	Stabilize/downturn
Spike	Maintain/fall
Surge	Plummet
Jump	Slump
Peak	Decline
Outpace	Fall behind

MULTI-LINE CHARTS CONVEY

Close	Move apart
Converge	Diverge
Move together	Separate
Tighten/overlap	Far apart

Use verbs similar to the ones on this page to describe how a line moves over time.

AN ADVERB MODIFIES A VERB IN RELATION TO CHANGE OVER TIME

To add clarity to your explanation of what the lines reveal in a chart, use an adverb in addition to a verb to describe the nature of the change over time or the relationship between the lines.

Describe how the slope of the line rises and falls using adverbs:

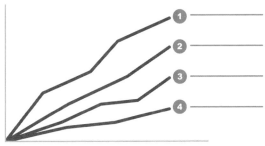

1 — Dramatically, sharply, rapidly, quickly, swiftly

2 — Substantially, considerably, significantly, consistently

3 — Moderately, markedly, slowly, gradually, steadily

4 — Slightly, fractionally, a little, minimally

For example, when you combine the verbs on the left page with the modifiers on this page, you might write these observations about a line in a chart.

Climbing dramatically

Slumping moderately

Plummeting quickly

Outpacing slightly

"Observation is a dying art."

STANLEY KUBRICK

Annotating Insights onto Charts

Overlay Visual Annotations onto a Chart

Our study of data slides uncovered an impressive set of methods my designers use for annotating charts. It delighted me to uncover the brilliance baked into their world-class designs. They have devised an ingenious range of simple visual elements to add to a chart as an additional layer to the data—like an overlay—to explain the most pertinent part.

Using visual annotations leads to quicker processing of the point you're making, in an elegant way. The annotations do two things: they may amplify a single point (highlight data or label data), or add math to data points (bracket data, delineate data, or explode data). The following pages show more ways to do both of these.

AMPLIFY A DATA POINT

HIGHLIGHT DATA

Choose a contrasting color so the main point stands out.

LABEL DATA

Create large, graphical labels to make one data point clear.

ADD MATH TO DATA POINTS

BRACKET DATA

Show differences or summations of data by showing some math.

DELINEATE DATA

Overlay a benchmark or goal line to draw attention to shortfalls and surpluses.

EXPLODE DATA

Break out deeper segmentation within a larger category.

TIP ▶ For a file of graphical annotations, go to duarte.com/datastory.

Amplify a
Data Point

HIGHLIGHT DATA

To make a piece of data stand out, put the secondary chart elements in a neutral or gray color, and use a pop of color for the plotted element you want the eye drawn to.

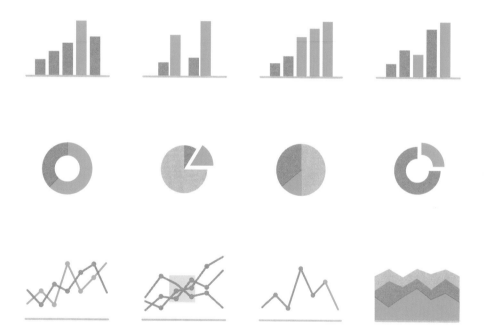

LABEL A DATA POINT

If you want to ensure a specific number in a chart is not overlooked, make that number huge. Combining the number with a graphical label is particularly effective.

TIP ▶ A donut is simply a pie chart with the most important segment annotated in the center.

Add Math
to Data Points

BRACKET DATA

Add brackets or boxes around data points you want to add math to. Visually connect two data points and then add, subtract, or calculate a multiple. Add pie segments together, or calculate the difference in height between two bars.

DELINEATE DATA

Use a line to demarcate a benchmark or goal. Then, show the math demonstrating how much above or below that goal you are. Lines can show the percentage to completion achieved, and highlight the amount left to go.

EXPLODE DATA

Categories of data often comprise subcategories, such as total sales broken down by region. A great way to highlight a subunit is to explode the details into a secondary chart.

Make Insights Visually Consumable

In my own firm, we have a great tool for aggregating and visualizing data, and one of the charts it generates is the bubble chart shown below. It represents the percentage of billable hours with the average hours per week on the vertical axis. The size of the bubbles represents a third data point, tracking how many non-billable hours each person puts in.

You can clearly see that there's a wide variance in the amount of non-billable time people are working. If a vertical line were added at the 75 percent billability mark, which is the employee's billability goal, you'd also quickly see bubbles representing those exceeding it. To me, though, the chart creates too much work to get to the insight. You have to roll over each bubble to see who is efficient or who has too much non-billable responsibility.

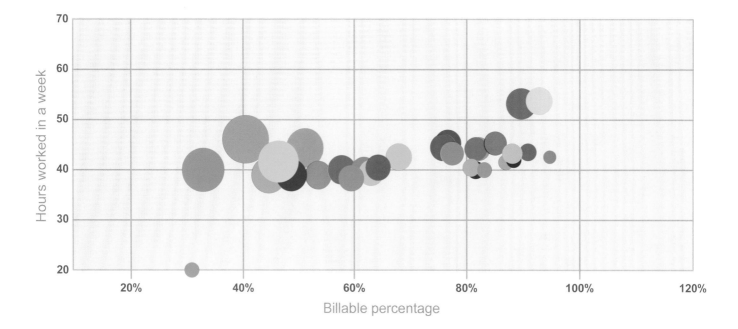

I asked our data analyst if he could make a new chart that would make the insights more self-evident. Could he annotate the insights he thought were particularly significant? He was up for the challenge, and generated the chart below.

I've changed the names of our team members, but his chart choice and insights are the same. He identified issues to address and he found that even though the highest-level staff were working significantly more hours, they were billing a lower percentage of their overall hours. One senior staff member had also seen a big drop off in billable time due to a promotion. The analyst gave me a clear recommendation to consider, and saved me the time of having to roll over a bunch of bubbles to get to the insights.

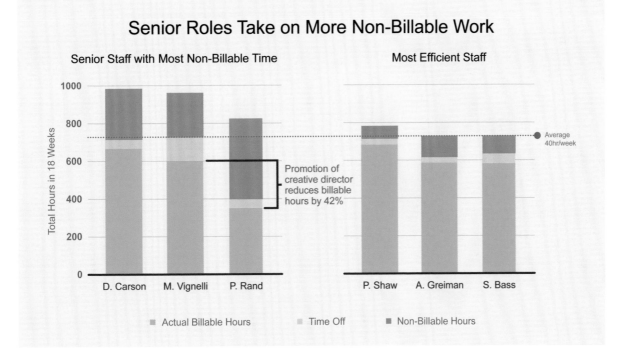

"A designer is an emerging synthesis of artist, inventor, mechanic, objective economist, and evolutionary strategist."

BUCKMINSTER FULLER

Building a
Skimmable Slidedoc

Build a Recommendation as a Slidedoc

In our time-strapped world, people prefer information that can be consumed quickly, with high confidence that the information is sound.

A Slidedoc is a visual document designed for quick consumption. It is intended to be read and distributed versus presented. You can create highly effective ones with presentation software. Many executives like receiving content in slide format, because it constrains the amount of detail you can provide. Chunking content into slides makes reading efficient, and encourages the author to exercise great discipline in terms of being concise. Below is a spectrum of visual artifacts created in organizations.

SPECTRUM OF CONTENT DENSITY

EXHAUSTIVE DOCUMENT

Deep research that proves a point.

Every department has some documentation that's necessarily long and dense, generally in the form of memos, reports, manuals, handbooks, and briefs. These artifacts present detailed information in a continuous linear format.

EXPLANATORY SLIDEDOC

Clear, skimmable recommendation.

This format should contain the right balance of detail and scanability to be used as a quick pre-read or handout. Slidedocs are authored in presentation software to combine the strengths of a document with the advantages of visualization.

PERSUASIVE PRESENTATION

Visual aid for verbal delivery.

Projected slides are a visual backdrop or stage setting that visually supports your verbal stream. Using visuals combines the power of the spoken word with compelling imagery that helps the audience remember what you've said.

Many executives say "send me five slides" when they want insights from you, and they are usually looking for a succinct Slidedoc to read. Because you won't be presenting it, a Slidedoc must contain enough meaty information to be a piece of standalone communication that can be consumed quickly.

The brain can only focus attention on one channel of information at a time: auditory or visual. An audience will either be listening to you speaking, or they will be reading. For this reason, you'd rarely (if ever) project a Slidedoc during a meeting or formal presentation. If you are asked to project a Slidedoc, don't speak when it is first displayed. Quietly let those in the room read it, and then host a conversation to drive consensus and decision around it.

Slidedocs are to be written with only one idea per slide, so each slide becomes its own standalone unit. This makes them modular, which means that slides can be easily cut and pasted into anyone else's deck. In fact, a fantastic Slidedoc is one of the best ways to spread your ideas. Good ones tend to rip around an organization because people find them so effective. This is a great way for your reputation to gain traction.

TIP ▶ If the people in your meeting didn't read your Slidedoc ahead of time, you can carve out 10 minutes or so at the beginning of the meeting to click silently through the deck, letting them read it. So people don't interrupt, ask them to withhold commentary, and instead write notes about feedback for discussion to follow.

Think of a Slidedoc as a Visual Book

Slidedocs borrow aspects from well-designed books and follow long-established formats. Books have a cover, table of contents, and chapter title pages to clearly announce their structure.

Because a Slidedoc is visual and skimmable, you can also think of them a bit like magazines, in which visual hierarchy is paramount. The components of a book that precede the main text are collectively called the *front matter*. First comes your cover page, which is an opportunity to convey a message right off the bat. How many times have you picked up a book just because it had a great title? The cover includes a title, your name, and the date of completion. The title and possible subtitle should be a tight, snappy version of your recommendation.

THE ANATOMY OF THE FRONT MATTER IN A SLIDEDOC

Title or Subtitle
As with book titles, your Slidedoc title should make others want to read it. Craft a clear DataPOV. Add a subtitle, if necessary, to help put a fine point on your topic.

Author's Name
Include your contact information under your name, so if the Slidedoc is shared widely, people can easily get in touch with you.

Date
Timeliness of information is a vital element of its relevance. Don't leave people guessing about how up to date your Slidedoc is.

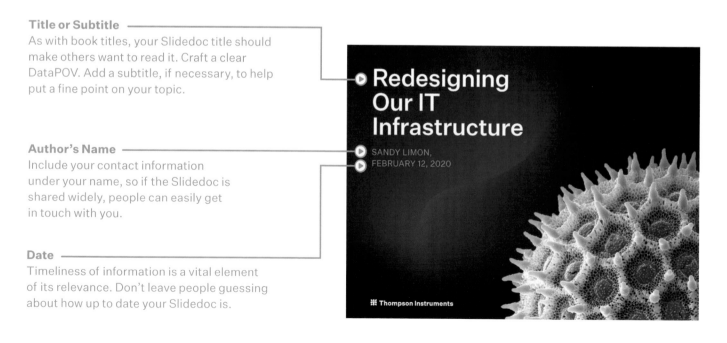

Your table of contents (TOC) allows your reader to get a quick overview of the structure and understand the gist of what the recommendation is about. You should also include page numbers so readers can jump to the sections they feel need the most attention from them. If the body of your Slidedoc is fewer than 10 slides, you might opt to forego a TOC.

Even though the TOC will be at the front of the Slidedoc, it should be the last thing you write. As you're working on the slides, their content and order will often evolve, so don't waste time putting slide numbers in a TOC until you know they won't change.

The next slide should be an executive summary. Don't use bullet points. Write text in full sentences to convey complete thoughts.

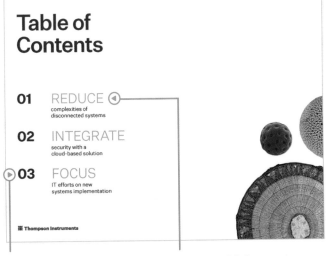

Page or Section Numbers
If you divided the Slidedoc into topical sections, include the section titles and page numbers for them.

Content Links
Each item in the TOC can include a hyperlink that allows readers to jump to that section.

Executive Summary
This should follow the three-act structure. Unpack the content as much as necessary for executives to understand it. Sometimes, this may be all they read.

Organize Content to Be Readable

For the layout of each slide, your content must be organized with a clear visual hierarchy that conveys what to read first and where to go from there.

The title and subtitle of most pages should be placed at the top left, in the largest type size. This is the default location for titles of slides in most presentation software. In Western society, we read from left to right continuously down the page, from top left to bottom right in a "Z" pattern.

Constructing page layouts so they facilitate this reading pattern, rather than fighting it, assists with the quick reading of a slide. Slidedocs should always be designed to be read from the top left of the slide to the bottom right of the last column.

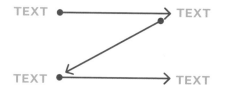

Slidedoc layouts consist of four elements: data, images, diagrams, and text. We have illustrated these four elements in the graphic below.

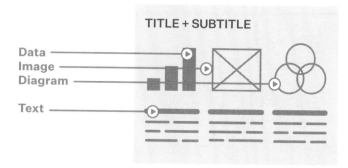

Notice the layouts on the right-hand page. The title stays in the standard/default place, but all of the pages look very different. The layouts show that you can divide a page into halves, thirds, or fourths. You can have up to six columns, though we don't recommend more than that.

2-COLUMN FORMAT
Page is visually split in half

3-COLUMN FORMAT
Page is visually split into thirds

4-COLUMN FORMAT
Page is visually split into fourths

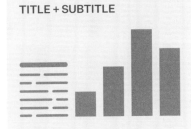

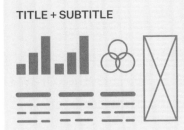

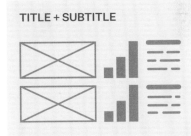

Deviate from Standard Format for Emphasis

In many slide decks we examined, panels were used to draw the eye to important content.

The previous pages featured examples of standard layouts with titles in the standard/default location.

By adding a vertical or horizontal color panel, key points can be emphasized. These are great for making elements very large, so they really pop, and for pithy summary text or key takeaways.

LEFT PANEL FOR TITLE AND SUBTITLES

For a slide title that needs to grab attention, you could use a panel on the left so your readers process it first. You can use this as the first slide in a section, or even in the middle of a section when a title needs special attention from readers.

BOTTOM AND RIGHT PANEL FOR KEY TAKEAWAYS

Because we read from top left to bottom right in a "Z" pattern, panels displaying summary text or key takeaway bullets should be at the bottom or on the right. This structures the slide to help readers fully understand the most important point.

SKETCHES OF LAYOUTS UTILIZING PANELS FOR EMPHASIS

Big Statistic
Panels are great for displaying numbers you want to make very large, so they really pop.

Emphasize Text That Must Be Read

Take the time to highlight sections of text on each page so readers notice the important bits. There are several ways to make text jump off a page. Magazines, newspapers, and websites have used these techniques for emphasizing text for decades. Below are examples of varying layouts for the same executive summary.

FIVE WAYS TO MAKE TEXT STAND OUT ON A PAGE

CHANGE TEXT ATTRIBUTES INLINE

Change the color or style (such as bold or italic) of the text within a sentence so it stands out. Red text is used in some Bibles for the words of Jesus.

MAKE TEXT LOOK HIGHLIGHTED

Place a color box behind the text, so it looks like a highlighter was used on the page. Use a light box behind dark text, or a dark box with white text.

BREAK THE GRID

When you have text that fits nicely in columns, one way to make text stand out is to format it so it breaks the boundaries of the columns.

OVERSIZED
QUOTATION MARKS

For text that is a quote, a nice device
is to make the quotation marks quite
large to signify its importance.

PLACE TEXT
WITHIN A SHAPE

Use a shape to place your text in.
It could be filled with a color, or you
could use lines to surround the shape.

TIP ▶ Go to Slidedocs.com for free
Slidedoc templates with beautiful
layouts and functionality already
designed for you.

Review the Anatomy of a Recommendation Tree

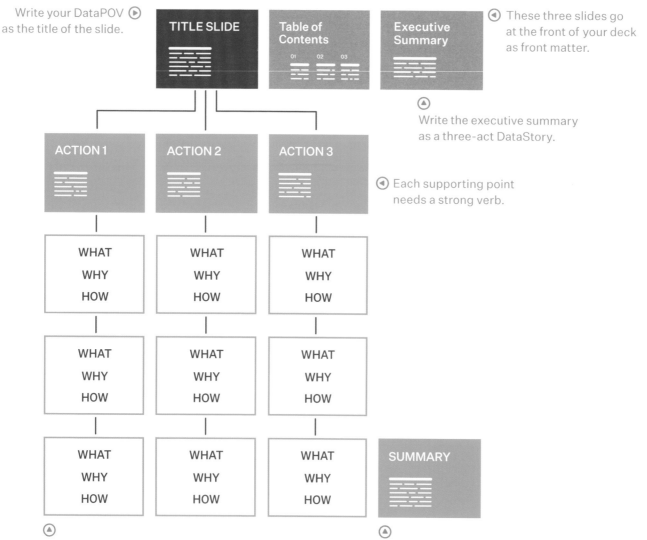

Write your DataPOV as the title of the slide.

TITLE SLIDE

Table of Contents
01   02   03

Executive Summary

These three slides go at the front of your deck as front matter.

Write the executive summary as a three-act DataStory.

ACTION 1

ACTION 2

ACTION 3

Each supporting point needs a strong verb.

WHAT
WHY
HOW

WHAT
WHY
HOW

WHAT
WHY
HOW

WHAT
WHY
HOW

WHAT
WHY
HOW

WHAT
WHY
HOW

WHAT
WHY
HOW

WHAT
WHY
HOW

WHAT
WHY
HOW

SUMMARY

Use just enough supporting slides to get your point across. Use What-Why-How to unpack your point.

Write a clear summary of the decision you are recommending.

If you were to print out your Slidedoc and paste it on the wall, it might look a lot like the structure on the left. If the recommendation requires extensive research, or has significant strategic implications, you may need many more slides than this.

PLACE ANY REFERENCE MATERIAL IN AN APPENDIX

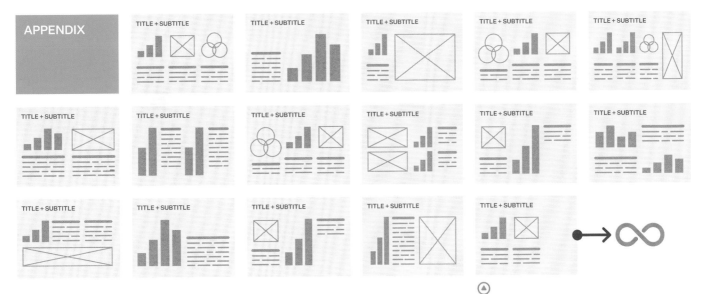

Use as many slides in the appendix as you'd like. Organize them clearly just in case your reader loves to peruse deeper data.

Review a Slidedoc as a Recommendation Tree

To the right is a Slidedoc written by an IT Director at Thompson Instruments to convince the executive team to fund the redesign of their IT infrastructure.

Notice how it has a slide title, table of contents, and executive summary. The recommendation is supported by three section heads. Each section head is supported by dense, yet skimmable, content answering What-Why-How.

"Good design is good business."

THOMAS WATSON, JR.
FORMER PRESIDENT OF IBM

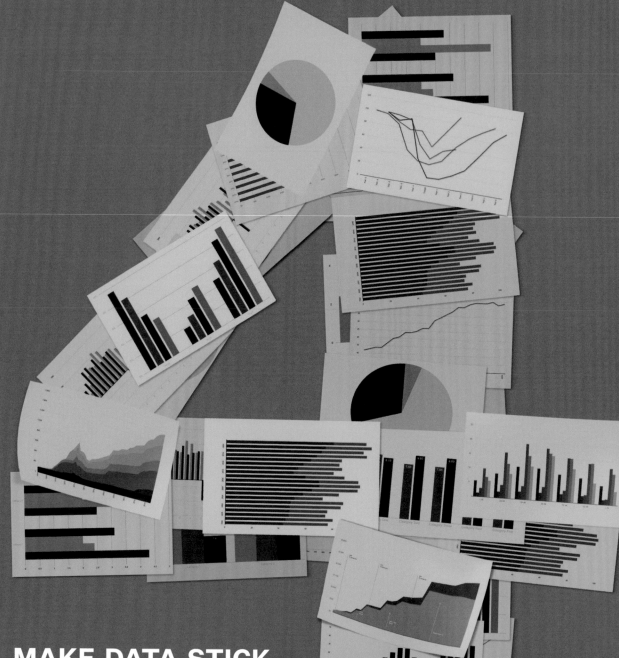

MAKE DATA STICK

CHAPTERS

IX.

Marveling at
the Magnitude

X.

Humanizing
Data

XI.

Storytelling
with Data

Marveling at the Magnitude

Attach the Data to Something Relatable

We use numbers at very large and very tiny scales that humans sometimes struggle to understand. How can we envision how large or small something is that we can't even see with the naked eye?

To help your audience understand the magnitude of the data, compare it to things that are familiar to them. When Jeff Bezos' net worth was abuzz in the news in 2018, Neil deGrasse Tyson tweeted:

> *" Not that anybody asked, but @JeffBezos' 130-billion dollars, laid end-to-end, can circle Earth 200 times then reach the Moon & back 15 times then, with what's left over, circle Earth another 8 times."* [18]

Wow, that sounds like a lot. But how far is the Moon, exactly? It's 238,000 miles. Okay, but that's hard to envision. Most of us mere mortals have never traveled that far in one trip. The longest plane flights we'll generally take are in the 10,000-mile range. If Tyson had said, "The thickness of 130 billion stacked one-dollar bills is 8,822 miles, which is equivalent to driving back and forth across the United States 3.4 times," the quantity would have been more comprehensible.

Another way to measure Bezos' wealth comes from *Forbes*. To determine his annual earnings, they calculated the difference between his 2017 and 2018 net worth. That figure was made more relatable by calculating it as an hourly wage, which was the staggering sum of $4,474,885, almost 157 times the median annual pay at Amazon of $28,466. Breaking the number down further, he made $74,581 per minute and $1,243 per second.[19]

Many of the numbers we use today are unfathomable in a tangible sense to the human mind. In 2004, Facebook hit 2 billion users. In 2018, Apple became the first public company with a net worth of $1 trillion. In December 2018, the U.S. national debt hit $21.97 trillion. How do we make sense of these sums?

Steve Jobs held new products close to his face. When they were projected onto huge screens, the audience could immediately grasp their size.

Develop a Sense of Scale

Data should always be precise. When trying to help others understand magnitude, though, exactitude isn't the point. You want to find an approximate comparison to convey the scale of the number quickly.

If you fixate on precision, you may want to skip this chapter. But you may also be one of those with the most to gain from it.

In the Bezos example of stacked dollar bills, you may find the U.S. Treasury's calculation of the thinness of a dollar bill (.0043 inches) to be an acceptable measurement. Or do you geek out about the teeny difference in the thickness of a newly-minted dollar bill as opposed to one that has been in circulation for a while? To grasp magnitude, it doesn't matter, because people have a sense of the thickness of a dollar.

THE COMMON WAYS PEOPLE SENSE SCALE

Helping others get their heads around how big or teeny a number is can be tricky. Make it clearer by comparing your number to things that are familiar and relatable to humans.

Size
Compare it to a relatable size

Distance
Compare it to a known distance

Time
Compare it to a segment of time

Speed
Compare it to how fast something travels

WAIT, WHERE'S THE SENSE OF WEIGHT?

Some measurements are trickier than others for finding good comparisons, because our minds struggle more to develop an intuitive sense of them.

WEIGHT

Even though weight is a common measurement in business, it isn't as relatable as things people can see. A sense of weight is created by the brain based roughly according to size, but as we've all experienced, size and weight do not always correlate as we expect. A large object might be fairly light. We also have trouble getting a sense for weight that is generally heavier than what we can pick up. You can hold a water bottle and perceive its weight, but could you comprehend the weight of a million water bottles? Probably not.*

HEIGHT

Height is a bit less relatable than length or distance. We have a sense of our own height, and that of things in fairly close relationship to our own eye level. For some heights, we get a sense of them because we see them often, and have probably been close to one: a telephone pole, a story of a building, a goal post. But as height increases above the range we're familiar with, we lose the ability to get an intuitive sense of it. Saying something is a mile high is not relatable unless you're a pilot, because there are no structures that tall to compare it to.

MICRO-MEASUREMENTS

In a world of micro-measurements, the difference between the width of a human hair and that of a piece of sand is vast. But we can't perceive that with our eyes, or even through our sense of touch. Unless your job has you gazing into a microscope often, comparing quantities at microscale will be mind-boggling. If you can say how many very tiny things would fit into something that is of relatable size, however, you can convey their scale fairly well. For example, in just one-fifth of a teaspoon of water, as many as 1 billion bacteria may be swimming around.[20] We get that they are really, really small.

Your readers will understand a number much better if they can see it or sense it rather than having to imagine how big it is. Even as you plot numbers on a chart, the axis of a scale can be hard to comprehend. Compare that scale to something relatable.

Based on a 16.9oz (500ml) Dasani water bottle with a 2.5 inch diameter, a million bottles fill three-quarters of a football field (or .7535204 of it, to be precise). It's easier to imagine that than to relate to how much it might weigh.

Connect Data to Relatable Size

Look around your environment right now, and compare the size of various things to one another. Try to find some that are about the same size, and some that are about half the size of others.

Now, imagine other familiar objects that aren't around you that are about those same sizes. Easy to do, right? We're good at this.

Many charts measure quantities. Convert quantities into sizes of other things. If a number on your axis is a million or more, convert it into the size of something. For example, if sales of your product dropped by a million units, maybe that much product would fill half of the glassy high-rise your sales team sits in. Or, a million dollars can be stacked or laid end-to-end to help others understand the scale of the quantity being plotted.

RELATABLE LENGTH

Length, Width, or Height
(also thickness or distance)

COMMON MEASUREMENTS
Linear inch, foot, yard, mile, centimeter, meter, kilometer.

EXAMPLES OF RELATABLE LENGTH
Your height, hand, or foot; an arm's length, a credit card, or the width of a car lane. Relatable distances are around a track, across a state, between two buildings, and from your house to work.

STATISTIC
In 2008, Steve Jobs launched the MacBook Air, claiming it was the "world's thinnest notebook" measuring 1.94 centimeters thick.

RELATABLE COMPARISON
During his presentation, Jobs pulled the computer out of an inter-office envelope to show just how thin it was.

RELATABLE AREA

Area
(length x width)

COMMON MEASUREMENTS

Square inch, foot, yard, acre, mile, centimeter, meter, kilometer.

EXAMPLES OF RELATABLE AREA

Football field, basketball court, city block, city limits. In Japan, the area of a room is expressed by the number of tatami mats it can accommodate, which are roughly three square feet. Places are usually measured in area.

STATISTIC

At more than 1.6 million square kilometers, the Great Pacific Garbage Patch is an ocean region where currents have collected a massive amount of plastic trash.[21]

RELATABLE COMPARISON

This huge, human-made disaster is twice the size of Texas.

RELATABLE VOLUME

Volume
(length x width x height)

COMMON MEASUREMENTS

Cubic inch, foot, yard, centimeter, meter.

EXAMPLES OF RELATABLE VOLUME

A building, stadium, Olympic swimming pool, shipping container, or plane. Things we can see and touch in a relatable way. For example, a blimp has a lot of volume, but it isn't as relatable as, say, an airplane.

STATISTIC

Apple's iPhone 6s packaging allowed 50 percent more units to be transported in an airline shipping container compared to the first-generation iPhone.

RELATABLE COMPARISON

Apple tied the statistic to fewer CO2 emissions by stating that the same shipment that used to require four cargo planes now shipped in two.[22]

Connect Data to Relatable Time

Time and speed are often related to one another in our lives, so they are good sources for comparison. For example, a good way to convey a distance is to say how long it would take to drive there at the familiar speed of a car or airplane, because time x speed = distance.

HOW LONG IT TAKES

 **Time**

COMMON MEASUREMENTS

Seconds, minutes, hours, days, months, years, decades. Very few can relate to the time scale of a century.

EXAMPLE OF RELATABLE TIMEFRAMES

Work hours, flights between cities, an episode of a sitcom, a TED talk, the time it takes to microwave popcorn, or boil an egg.

STATISTIC

Our complex data takes anywhere from 23 to 26 hours to process.

RELATABLE COMPARISON

With the old process of pulling complex data from our systems, it took the same amount of time as it would to fly from New York City to Sydney, and then you'd have to wait a bit for it to finish. With improvement in the process, it is now equivalent to flying from New York City to Los Angeles.

HOW FAST IT GOES

 **Speed**
(distance x time)

COMMON MEASUREMENTS

Number of miles per hour, or amount of time to travel to various places.

EXAMPLE OF RELATABLE SPEED

Blinking, walking, speed limits, a roller coaster ride. Speeds that are harder to understand are milliseconds or clock cycles of a CPU.

STATISTIC

The Moon is 268,000 miles away, but how far is that, really?

RELATABLE COMPARISON

According to cosmologist Fred Hoyle, if you drove a car upward at 60 mph, in about an hour, you'd be in space. To get to the Moon, it'd take 4,000 hours of nonstop driving (or almost half a year).[23] By the way, the distance to the Sun is 92.96 million miles, and it would take 177 years at 65 mph to get there.

MIX AND MATCH COMPARING SIZE, TIME, AND DISTANCE

It is most common to sense scale through quantity, size, distance, time, and speed. So, mixing and matching these measures is another way to make a number feel relatable.

COMPARE WITH SIZE (AREA)

- **Measurement:** The tiny aqua bullet point at the beginning of this sentence is 1/20th (.05) of a square inch, or 1.27 millimeters.

- **Comparison:** One million squares would fill almost 31 pages. A billion fills 30,864 pages, and a trillion? 30,864,197 pages, which makes a book nearly 1.22 miles thick.

COMPARE WITH TIME

- **Measurement:** One million seconds is 11.57 days, a billion seconds is 31.7 years, and a trillion seconds is 31,688 years.

- **Comparison:** If you spend $1 million per day starting from year zero, it'd take until the year 2740 to get to $1 trillion.

COMPARE WITH DISTANCE

- **Measurement:** One millimeter is roughly the thickness of a paper clip, guitar string, or credit card, which seems pretty small.

- **Comparison:** A million millimeters is one kilometer (about 12 New York City blocks); a billion is 1,000 km, 150 times the length of the Las Vegas Strip (4.2 miles, or 6.8 km); and a trillion millimeters is 621,371 miles, which would circle the globe 25 times.

In our courses, we have people come up with all sorts of crazy comparisons for data. For example, one attendee calculated the following: "If every meeting at LinkedIn started as late as the recommended time for brushing your teeth, we would be overstaffed by almost 1,250 people." Another calculated in her data that she could binge-watch all 552 episodes of *The Simpsons* while comparing her data to time.

Compare Data to Relatable Things

In addition to using size, time, and speed to understand a number, you can also compare various nouns (people, places, things) to one another to comprehend quantity and scale.

COMPARING ITEMS OF RELATABLE SIZE

If you're showing the scale of a physical object, try placing an item near it that is familiar to your audience. Placing things in proximity to each other, whether in, on, under, next to, or in front of other items, helps make the scale clear.

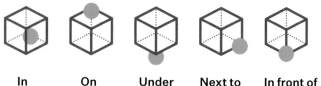

In **On** **Under** **Next to** **In front of**

Describing the number of people who could fit inside of something can help people understand a number. Employees, customers, patients, and students commonly inhabit things like vans, buses, planes, buildings, arenas, hospitals, or stadiums.

Let's say you have 1 million users. It's easier for an audience to get a sense of that quantity if you compare it to the number of people who could be seated in a stadium. For example, the San Francisco Giants' baseball field has 41,915 seats. So, you could say: "Our users would fill the San Francisco Giants' stadium almost 24 times." For you precision geeks, the exact math is 23.85780746749374 times—see how helpful approximation can be!

Instead of using dimensions or quantity of megabytes to describe the first iPod, Steve Jobs compared it to the size of a pocket—a very familiar thing.

> *"I happen to have one right here in my pocket. This amazing little device holds a thousand songs, and it goes right in my pocket."* —Steve Jobs

Express How You Feel About the Data

Let your emotions about outcomes show. If an important number spikes up, celebrate that. If it tanks, acknowledge how upsetting that is.

EMOTIVE WORDS AND PHRASES

Use phrases that show what you feel. "Isn't that incredible?" "How fantastic!" "I think we've gotten the company we all care so much about back on track, and that feels very, very good." "This is sad. Really, really sad."

SOUNDS THAT REFLECT EMOTION

You can vocalize the sounds a chart would make if it were a moving object making a noise on impact, or screeching sounds when it changes direction suddenly. Steve Jobs used the word "boom" 79 times in his public keynotes when he was excited about the speed of a product demo.

- **Explosions:** Boom, Bang, Pop
- **Collisions:** Crash, Bang, Clash, Wham, Smack, Whomp, Whump, Thump, Bump
- **High Speed:** Zoom, Whoosh, Swoosh, Zing

INTERJECTIONS

These are short exclamations of an emotion. They're great for dramatic effect, and we'll come back to them later.

POSITIVE INTERJECTIONS[24]

Relief: Ahhh, Oh, Phew, Whew

Achievement: Aha, Boo-yah, Hurrah, Yay

Impressed: Whee, Whoopee, Woo-hoo, Yippee

Surprise: Ah, Uh-oh, Whaaat?, Whoa, Yikes

Awe: Awww, Wow, Wowie, Yowza

NEGATIVE INTERJECTIONS

Disappointment: Ack, Drats, Ew, Gak, Ugh, Yuck

Disdain: Blech, Ewww, Ick, Phooey, Pee-yew

Frustration: Argh, Dang, Eek, Grrr, Gosh, Oy, Sheesh

Mockery: Boo-hoo, Duh, Whoop-de-doo

RHETORICAL QUESTION

Asking a question is a subtle form of persuasion to help the audience think about a point you're making.

As a student of great speeches, I've transcribed every public talk Steve Jobs ever delivered. He often asked rhetorical questions to engage an audience.

STEVE JOBS

" iMac, as you know, started shipping on August 15th, and through the end of the year, how many iMacs did we ship? **<rhetorical question>** *We shipped a wonderful number* **<emotive words>** *we shipped 800,000 of them. 800,000 iMacs in four and a half months. Now, if you do the math, that equals one every 15 seconds of every minute of every hour of every day of every week. In that time period, an iMac was sold somewhere in the world.* **<relatable time>** *We are thrilled with this.* **<emotive words>** *It's made iMac the number-one-selling computer model in America, and we are very happy.* **<emotive words>** *"*

BONO

In the *LA Times* report on Bono's 2013 TED talk, Bono presented statistics about how those living in "soul-crushing poverty" had fallen from 43 percent in 1990 to 21 percent in 2010. He exclaimed...

" If the trajectory continues, look where the amount of people living on $1.25 a day gets to by 2030. Can't be true, can it? **<rhetorical question>** *If the trajectory continues, we get to, wow* **<interjection>**, *the zero zone.* *"*

Bono ran through statistics showing progress made in combating extreme poverty. The first statistic showed that mortality rates for kids under five had fallen so much that 7,256 fewer children were dying each day.

" Have you read anything, anywhere that's as remotely as important as that number? **<rhetorical question>** *...It drives me nuts that people don't seem to know that.* **<emotive words>** *"* [25]

"Things on a very small scale behave like nothing that you have any direct experience about. They do not behave like waves, they do not behave like particles, they do not behave like clouds, or billiard balls, or weights on springs, or like anything that you've ever seen."

RICHARD P. FEYNMAN
PHYSICIST

Humanizing Data

Meet the Hero and Adversary of the Data

Some data has nothing to do with humans, but most does. Most organizational data wouldn't exist without humans generating it. We are buying and selling goods, clicking on links, wearing devices, undergoing medical tests, selling homes, etc. You can find life experiences within the data of almost every chart.

Empathetically understanding the people whose actions generate your data helps guide you to better communicate with them. Think of them as characters in your DataStory. They either help the organization achieve your goals, or contribute to falling short of them. They are, in other words, either heroes or adversaries of your data.

HERO   **ADVERSARY**

**Plays a role in moving the data in a
desirable direction.**

**Obstructs attainment of a goal or creates
a problem the hero must solve.**

In storytelling, a hero usually has a goal or desire they'd
like to fulfill. Understanding those goals and desires
will help you assist the hero in achieving them.

The adversary thwarts the hero, or has a competing goal
the hero must prevent the adversary from achieving. They
throw roadblocks in the way of achieving the goal.

Could be a customer, user, employee,
partner, donor, voter, patient.

Could be competitors, the media, an
activist, investor, a mindset.

Heroes that drive a number up   Adversaries that drive a number down

High-performing employees	⟶ > ⟶	Inefficient process or bureaucracy
Generous donors to nonprofits	⟶ > ⟶	Changes in tax laws
Early adopters of new products	⟶ > ⟶	Vindictive influencers or reporters
Exceeding assigned quota	⟶ > ⟶	Emergence of clever competitors
Users on a website	⟶ > ⟶	User experience glitches

Know the Adversary in the Data

You identify the adversary by understanding the type of conflict your hero is experiencing. Below are classic types of conflict found in myths, stories, and movies to help you understand your hero.

FIVE TYPES OF STORY CONFLICT IN DATA

CONFLICT TYPES	FAMOUS MOVIES	DEFINITION
Hero vs. Self	*Rocky, The Shawshank Redemption*	Conflict is with character's own flaws, doubts, or prejudices.
Hero vs. Person	*Batman, The Da Vinci Code*	Conflict is with another character.
Hero vs. Society	*Hunger Games, Erin Brokovich*	Conflict is with beliefs and actions of a social group that go against your values.
Hero vs. Technology	*The Matrix, Wall Street*	Conflict is with technology or systems that become a negative influence.
Hero vs. Nature	*Jaws, Twister*	Conflict is with a problem related to nature.

ADVERSARY

Hero vs. fear, morals (greed, pride), values, self-image, mindset, bias, self-management, etc.

Hero vs. employee, customer, user, investor, regulator, authority figure, analyst, activist, politician, criminal, etc.

Hero vs. institutions, competitor, market, team, shareholders, news, traditions, regulation, cultural norms, management, etc.

Hero vs. technology, systems, process, computer virus, etc.

Hero vs. disease, natural disasters, unclean drinking water, etc.

The hero in your data could be in conflict with a person, group, way of thinking, or system that creates a roadblock for them. Roadblocks come in many shapes, such as fear, bureaucracy, technology, bias, and even cancer cells.

The way you communicate can rally the hero to overcome an adversary pushing data in an undesirable direction.

Address the
Conflict in the Data

Data isn't just a set of numbers. Each data point can offer insight into people and their conflicts. Sometimes, the adversary isn't self-evident. Using the five types of conflict on the previous page, let's see how they can help you empathize with a data hero.

Notice in the chart on the right that upgrades have stalled. But why? In this chart, the customers are the hero on a journey, and some adversarial force is stopping the upgrades from growing. By talking to customers, you get insights into the type of conflict they are facing. The conflict they are experiencing should be addressed by you when you communicate with them, so they are emboldened to overcome it. In the scenarios on the right, the type of conflict has been identified, and will shape how you communicate with them.

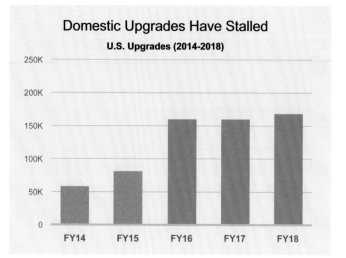

Domestic Upgrades Have Stalled
U.S. Upgrades (2014-2018)

SCENARIO:

CUSTOMERS AREN'T UPGRADING

Your hero is almost always the customer, and your desired goal, in this case, is for them to upgrade. Let's call this customer "Fran." Identify Fran's adversary to understand the nature of the issues she's confronting, and discover ways to motivate her to overcome these roadblocks.

HERO	ADVERSARY	TYPES OF CONFLICT
Fran is considering upgrading her phone.	Her carrier doesn't have the phone she wants.	Fran vs. company
	The reservation process is inconvenient.	Fran vs. technology
	She isn't confident it's time to upgrade.	Fran vs. self

Fran's trying to decide if she should upgrade her phone. She's grappling with three sources of conflict that are stopping her, and each requires a different means of resolution. Motivating her must therefore involve multiple approaches.

SCENARIO:

SALES ARE DOWN

The data adversary is often some aspect of the company's own product, services, or processes. We have all felt like we were battling an organization at some point. Here's what might be happening when you discover your sales are down.

HERO	ADVERSARY	TYPES OF CONFLICT
The sales team is working harder than any other year.	Sales management isn't appreciating the effort.	Team vs. company
	38 percent of deals have been lost due to new pricing model.	Team vs. system
	New sales leader scored low in pulse survey.	Team vs. person

The go-to explanation for low sales is to examine marketing's effort. In the case above, the adversary of the data is how the sales department is being managed.

Resolving the conflict may only require a minor adjustment, or it may take a herculean effort by the entire company. By identifying the type of conflict, you will get a clearer view of the roadblocks the organization must remove to get heroes unstuck.

Speak with the Characters

Data tells you what has happened in the past, but doesn't always tell you why unless you talk to the heroes generating the data or the adversaries against it.

You may uncover the fact that an increasing number of customers are abandoning shopping carts before online purchase… but why? That users are churning, but why? That profit is down, but why? That employee retention is up, but why? That clients didn't return, but why?

The chart to the right shows that sales are down. You can't help improve sales until you understand the impediments driving it down. You might focus on the sales pitch or the pricing, but what if the problem is the sales manager? Maybe he's great at sucking up to you, but is sucking the lifeblood out of his team.

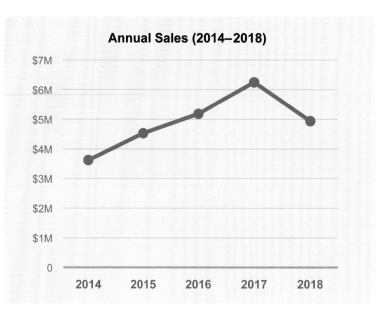

To help your hero get unstuck, go straight to the source! Read forums and conduct surveys, or hire consultants to learn what stands in their way. Also make use of whatever user or customer comments you have access to. Read hundreds of them to acutely understand what it's like to walk in their shoes. Sometimes, you can catch problems this way before they become widespread. **Even one stray comment you read may show early signs of a problem or opportunity.**

The best way to really understand your heroes and learn about their issues is to speak with a number of them. There's nothing more valuable for acutely perceiving their needs, desires, and problems than a good old-fashioned two-way conversation. Identify a random sampling of data heroes and speak with them, asking about concerns, opinions, and motivations. Talking to them reveals their adversary in a way quantitative data can't.

Listen deeply to them, and ask open-ended questions so you don't restrict what they might tell you. Rather than "Is the price stopping you from buying?" ask "Can you share what's stopping you from buying?" Also, turn the conversation around, by letting them ask you questions.

That's a powerful way to reveal things on their mind you might never have thought of. People open up when they feel someone cares.

With deep understanding of your heroes and adversaries, you can communicate your recommendation from an empathetic place, and make it more relevant to them.

With such powerful technological tools for probing into data, it's easy to lose sight of the fact that it represents the desires, pursuits, and problems of individual people.

It's only by understanding the human story the data has to tell, that you can craft a story of your own to drive your heroes to desired outcomes.

Share Context to Add Meaning to Data

By attaching meaning to a bit of abstract data, people create a scene of their life for us. They craft a mini-narrative. These stories and scenes are memorable—at least the good ones are.

When we attach meaning to a data point, we bring it to life and make it memorable.

At the beginning of each of our DataStory workshops, facilitators ask half the attendees to state one statistic that is important to them. Their answers sound like this: 7, 22, 57, 92, 1959, etc. The other half of the room is asked to state a statistic, and also to share why it is meaningful to them. Their answers sound like this: "Three. Because three people in my family share the same birthday."

"Forty-eight is the average number of hours I work per week." "$72,000 is the amount of debt I have." "Nine is the age I was when I thought I was a magical princess." At the end of the day, we ask the class which statistics they can recall, and almost all associated with personal meaning are remembered. For the others, only a small fraction is recalled.

CONTEXT CREATES MEANING

The chart below shows the number of young men living at home, and can be perceived as negative or positive depending upon the situation of the young men's lives.

This trend has been covered in the media as a negative reflection on young men, assuming they're immature. But what if the cost of renting a starter apartment has spiked significantly, and your kid's entire paycheck would go to cover rent?

Living with one's parents suddenly seems a great way to save, and maybe have more money to pay down student debt. Maybe some of these young men are industrious entrepreneurs, and they want to pour every ounce of their income into their startup. Understanding the context of a hero's life is vital to knowing the type of conflict they're dealing with.

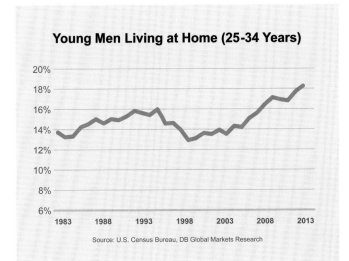

Young Men Living at Home (25-34 Years)

Source: U.S. Census Bureau, DB Global Markets Research

Save Lives with Data
Case Study: Dr. Rosalind Picard

Dr. Picard delivered a TEDx talk on how data collected from a smart watch can predict when someone may have a seizure. You may be surprised who the hero in the story is.

In addition to being a professor of media arts and sciences at MIT, Picard is the founder and director of the Affective Computing Research Group at the MIT Media Lab and co-founder of the startups Affectiva and Empatica.

Picard helped develop a cutting-edge smartwatch that can detect side effects from epileptic seizures before they occur, and alert nearby loved ones in time to help.

Her TEDxBeaconStreet talk, *An AI Smartwatch that Detects Seizures,* is on TED.com.

"This is Henry, a cute boy, and when Henry was three, his mom found him having some febrile seizures. Febrile seizures are seizures that occur when you also have a fever, and the doctor said, 'Don't worry too much. Kids usually outgrow these.' When he was four, he had a convulsive seizure, the kind when you lose consciousness and shake—a generalized tonic-clonic seizure—and while the diagnosis of epilepsy was in the mail, Henry's mom went to get him out of bed one morning, and as she went in his room, she found his cold, lifeless body.

Henry died of SUDEP, sudden unexpected death in epilepsy. I'm curious how many of you have heard of SUDEP. **<Very few hands are raised>** This is a very well-educated audience, and I see only a few hands. SUDEP is when an otherwise healthy person with epilepsy dies, and they can't attribute it to anything they can find in an autopsy. **There is a SUDEP every seven to nine minutes. That's on average two per TED talk.**

ⓐ **Marvel at the Magnitude**
Picard used the comparison of a familiar time (the length of a TED talk) to help them understand the scale of the quantity of deaths.

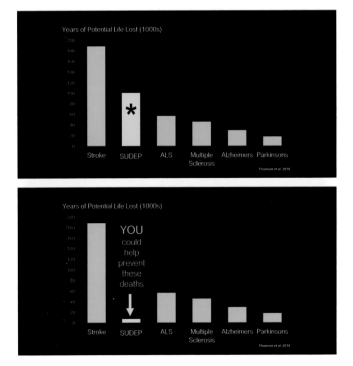

There are more SUDEPs in the United States every year than sudden infant death syndrome. **Now, how many of you have heard of sudden infant death syndrome? Pretty much every hand goes up.**

▲ **Compare Quantity**
  She had the audience visually demonstrate how many knew about SUDEP versus SIDS by having them raise their hands.

So, what's going on here? Why is this so much more common, and yet people haven't heard of it? And what can you do to prevent it?

Even though most of you have never heard of SUDEP, it is actually the number two cause of years of potential life lost of all neurological disorders.

The vertical axis is the number of deaths times the remaining life span, so higher is much worse impact.

SUDEP, however, unlike these others, is something that people right here could do something to push that down.

▲ **Meet the Hero**
  You may have thought that the hero of the story is the child fighting the disease, Henry, and he is heroic. But Picard is making the audience the heroes of her story, because they are the ones who can help stop deaths in the future.

○ This sweatband has a home-built, skin-conductance sensor inside of it.

▼ **Storytelling with Data**
  Picard tells the story of the data adversary.

One day, one of our undergrads knocked on my door at the end of the December semester, and he said: 'Professor Picard, can I please borrow one of your wristband sensors? My little brother has autism, he can't talk, and I want to see what's stressing him out.'

And I said: 'Sure. In fact, don't just take one, take two,' because they broke easily back then.

Now, I was back at MIT, looking at the data on my laptop, and the first day, I thought, 'Hmm, that's odd, he put them on both wrists instead of waiting for one to break. Okay, fine, don't follow my instructions.' I'm glad he didn't.

A few more days ahead, one wrist signal was flat, and the other had the biggest peak I've ever seen, and I thought, 'What's going on? We've stressed people out at MIT in every way imaginable. I've never seen a peak this big.' And it was only on one side. How can you be stressed on one side of your body and not the other? So, I thought one or both sensors must be broken. I started a whole bunch of stuff to try to debug this, and long story short, I could not reproduce this.

So I resorted to old-fashioned debugging. I called the student at home on vacation. 'Hi, how's your little brother? How's your Christmas? Hey, do you have any idea what happened to him?'

⊕ **Humanize Data**
Interview the characters making the numbers go up or down.

And I gave this particular date and time, and the data. And he said, 'I don't know, I'll check the diary.' Diary? An MIT student keeps a diary? So I waited, and he came back. He had the exact date and time, and he says,

'That was right before he had a grand mal seizure.'

At the time, I didn't know anything about epilepsy, and did a bunch of research. I realized that another student's dad was chief of neurosurgery at Children's Hospital Boston, screwed up my courage, and called Dr. Joe Madsen.

'Hi, Dr. Madsen. Is it possible somebody could have a huge sympathetic nervous system surge (that's what drives skin conductance) 20 minutes before a seizure?'

And he says, 'Probably not.' He says: 'It's interesting. We've had people whose hair stands on end on one arm 20 minutes before a seizure.'

And I'm like, 'On one arm?' I didn't want to tell him that initially, because I thought this was too ridiculous.

I showed him the data. We made a bunch more devices, and got them safety certified. Ninety families were enrolled in a study, all with children who were going to be monitored 24/7.

But we also learned some other things about SUDEP during this. One thing we learned was that SUDEP, when it happens, doesn't happen during the seizure, and it doesn't usually happen immediately afterwards; but when the person just seems very still and quiet, they may go into another phase where breathing stops, and then after the breathing stops, later, the heart stops.

Now, the next slide is what made my skin conductance go up. **One morning, I'm checking my email, and I see a story from a mom who said she was in the shower, and her phone was on the counter by the shower, and it said her daughter might need her help. So she interrupts her shower and goes running to her daughter's bedroom, and she finds her daughter face down in bed, blue and not breathing. She flips her over—human stimulation—and her daughter takes a breath, and another breath, and her daughter turns pink and is fine.**

Ⓐ **Storytelling with Data**
   Tell stories of how data helped individuals change outcomes.

We got another alert this morning, ran to her room and **she was face down with a seizure/not breathing!**

We **repositioned** her and she is now pink and sleeping.

Another is her family and the wonderful people out there who want to be there to support people who have conditions they've felt uncomfortable in the past mentioning to others. And the other reason is all of you, because we have the opportunity to shape the future of AI. We can actually change it, because we are the ones building it.

So, let's build AI that makes everybody's lives better."

Meet the Hero
When data alerted Natasha's mom that she needed stimulation, her daughter breathed again. Picard wants you to know that you can save a life, too. SUDEP is the adversary, and you can be the hero.

I think I turned white reading this email. My first response was: 'Oh, no, it's not perfect. The Bluetooth could break, the battery could die. All these things could go wrong. Don't rely on this.'

And she said, 'It's okay. I know no technology is perfect. None of us can always be there all the time. But this, this device plus AI enabled me to get there in time to save my daughter's life.'

Why do all this hard work to build AIs? A couple of reasons here: One is Natasha, the girl who lived, and her family wanted me to tell you her name.

"You cannot hope to build a better world without improving the individuals. To that end, each of us must work for his own improvement, and, at the same time, share a general responsibility for all humanity, our particular duty being to aid those to whom we think we can be most useful."

MARIE CURIE
PHYSICIST, CHEMIST, AND NOBEL PRIZE WINNER

Storytelling with Data

Leverage the Temporal Dimension When Presenting Data

Now that you've determined what others need to do, you may be the one asked to influence them to believe it is doable and inspire them to action.

Almost every recommendation requires a group of people to execute it, whether that's peers in your department, the executive team, or a broader audience. If you need to influence a department, customer, shareholder, or the entire company, you'll likely be asked to give a formal presentation.

When you have the stage, you can use cinematic design and storytelling techniques to make a presentation dynamic, revealing insights in a dramatic fashion. Make your DataStory truly come alive by creating suspense and telling an intriguing story with some elements of mystery. By strategically withholding key features of your findings at first, you can give the audience an exciting jolt of surprise with a big reveal.

Let's say your team has worked very hard, and you're about to present the results. You can create suspense by having each bar in a chart revealed one at a time. If the team is unaware of the final outcome, this lets you set up how messy it's been, and how hard they have worked. Then the team rejoices when they see the final, positive outcome.

HITCHCOCK EXPLAINS THE DIFFERENCE BETWEEN SURPRISE AND SUSPENSE

" *There is a distinct difference between 'suspense' and 'surprise,' and yet many pictures continually confuse the two. I'll explain what I mean.*

We are now having a very innocent little chat. Let's suppose that there is a bomb underneath this table between us. Nothing happens, and then all of a sudden, 'Boom!' There is an explosion. The public is surprised, but prior to this surprise, it has seen an absolutely ordinary scene, of no special consequence.

Now, let us take a suspense situation. The bomb is underneath the table and the public knows it, probably because they have seen the anarchist place it there. The public is aware the bomb is going to explode at one o'clock, and there is a clock in the decor. The public can see that it is a quarter to one. In these conditions, the same innocuous conversation becomes fascinating because the public is participating in the scene.

The audience is longing to warn the characters on the screen: 'You shouldn't be talking about such trivial matters. There is a bomb beneath you, and it is about to explode!'

In the first case, we have given the public 15 seconds of surprise at the moment of the explosion. In the second, we have provided them with 15 minutes of suspense. The conclusion is that whenever possible, the public must be informed. Except when the surprise is a twist; that is, when the unexpected ending is, in itself, the highlight of the story."

— *Alfred Hitchcock*

REVEAL HIDDEN DATA

Surprise is the feeling we get when something unexpected happens suddenly.

- **Add context to the data**

- **Zoom in or out of the data**

TELL A STORY WITH DATA

Suspense is the feeling of anticipation that builds while the outcome of a story is unclear.

- **Data ending in ill fortune**

- **Data ending in good fortune**

Reveal Hidden Data

You've probably been surprised by a story and physically reacted with a gasp of awe, or shudder of horror, as you empathize with a character encountering the unexpected. Data revealed over time elicits similar reactions from an audience.

A negative surprise can provoke a gasp of shock, while a positive surprise can create a gasp of awe, or applause.

TWO WAYS TO SURPRISE AN AUDIENCE

- **Add context to the data:** Report additional information that gives your data a strikingly different meaning.

- **Zoom in or out of the data:** Reveal a hidden feature of a chart or axis that shows an unexpected result.

The audience will enjoy a pleasant surprise, or people may be angered by negative surprises. This might sound bad, but in moving people to take action, anger can be an extremely powerful force, especially when people feel confident that they have the power to make change happen.

ADD CONTEXT TO THE DATA

When shown the chart below, the audience concludes that the number of U.S. jobs requiring artificial intelligence (AI) skills has been growing quickly.[26]

The chart below adds the context of other countries' data, which, when revealed after the first chart, shows that U.S. growth has been comparatively puny.

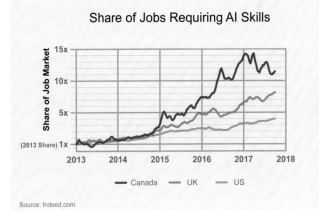

Note that the scale of the y-axis had to be adjusted by almost three times to accommodate the new data.

Reveal Hidden Data
(continued)

ZOOM IN OR OUT OF THE DATA

To the right are two slides. The bottom slide only shows part of the *y*-axis. That bottom slide is shown first. Then, using a push transition in PowerPoint®, the blue bars appear to grow and grow. Start reading the script labeled with the green number one below, and continue to read the script counterclockwise as the chart emerges over time.

① Only red bars are projected

"People assume that America's debt problems come from wasteful spending. This is just not true. In fact, over the past 30 years, families have cut a lot of their spending. Adjusted for inflation, the average family is spending less on food, including eating out; less on clothing, less on furniture, less on appliances than they did a generation ago. The numbers are pretty conclusive on this. Today, the data show that most American families watch their nickels…"

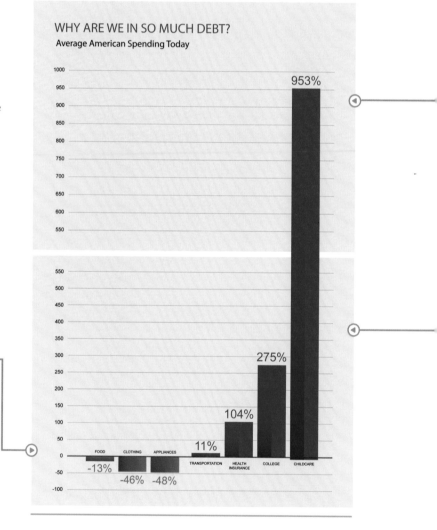

TIP ▶ Animated slide is at duarte.com/datastory.

(3) The slide appears to grow as more of the axis is revealed that exceeds the height of the slide

" Wow, there we go. <gasp in audience> It is no wonder that American families have blown through their savings and are taking on debt."

(2) Blue bars appear when clicked

"But boy, have they gotten slammed by the big stuff. The big, fixed expenses are truly staggering. Families today spend 57 percent more on their mortgages—this is all adjusted for inflation—and 104 percent more on health insurance. College, even at a state school, is through the roof. A kid today will pay tuition and fees nearly three times higher than in the 1970s. (The bar for childcare costs begins to grow) With more parents of small children headed into the workforce for long hours, the cost of childcare is enough to rock any family. In fact, see what happens to it?"

Reveal Hidden Data
Case Study: Al Gore

Who would have thought a movie about a slideshow full of data would win an Academy Award? During the documentary *An Inconvenient Truth*, the producers revealed data in an unprecedented way. Former U.S. Vice President Al Gore delivered the presentation in a small studio in Southern California. The producers commissioned a custom, 90-foot-wide, digital screen for the movie,[27] and Mr. Gore stunned the audience with a startling reveal.

The primary screen was so big that Gore had to get on a scissor lift to point to a rising red line depicting the increase in atmospheric carbon dioxide levels predicted for future years. As the line ascended higher and higher, the audience could see the end of the rise was imminent when a yellow dot was displayed. After all, the screen only went so high. What they didn't know was that the production team had built a secret screen above the 90-foot screen, which was hidden behind the stage drapery. The audience gasped as Gore continued to ascend on the lift as the extra screen was revealed, showing the shocking additional rise in carbon dioxide all the way to 2056.

We call this a S.T.A.R. moment, which stands for Something They'll Always Remember. A S.T.A.R. moment can't be kitschy, or it could come off as a cheesy summer camp skit. The moment must be in keeping with the overall tone of your presentation. You are seeking to draw attention to the significance of surprising data, and you don't want theatrics to distract from it.

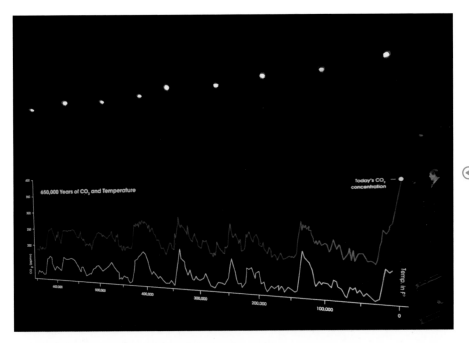

◉ Al Gore used a scissor lift to show just how high the number had risen.

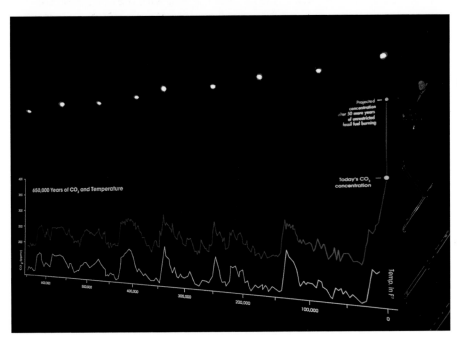

◉ The audience gasped when Gore continued to climb to an even higher statistic.

Tell a Story with an Emotional Arc
Case Study: Kurt Vonnegut

Kurt Vonnegut was an American novelist best known for his book *Slaughterhouse-Five* (1969). In this transcript of a lecture, he was questioning why computers couldn't process the simple shape of stories. The illustrations are those he drew on a chalkboard as he lectured.

"There's no reason why the simple shapes of stories can't be fed into computers. They are beautiful shapes.

This is the G-I axis: good fortune, ill fortune. Sickness and poverty down here, wealth and boisterous good health up there. Here's the very middle. Now, this is the B-E axis. B stands for beginning, E stands for electricity (laughter). Now, this is an exercise in relativity. It is the shape of the curves that matters, and not their origins.

A little above average...we call this story 'Man in a Hole,' but it needn't be about a man, and it needn't be somebody getting into a hole. But it's a good way to remember. Somebody gets into trouble, and gets out of it again. People love that story; they never get sick of it.

MAN IN A HOLE

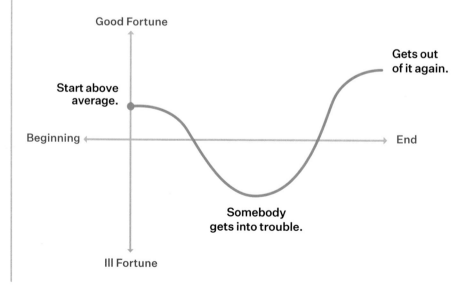

Another story is called 'Boy Gets Girl.' Start on an average day; the average person not expecting anything to happen. A day like any other. Finds something wonderful, just loves it. Oh, goddamnit! Got it back again. People like that.

BOY GETS GIRL

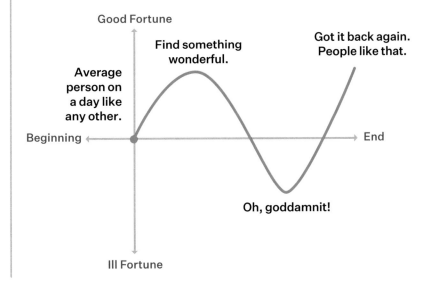

Computers can now play chess, so I don't know why they can't digest this very difficult curve I'm going to draw for you now. And it just so happens that this is the most popular story in Western civilization. Every time it's retold, somebody makes another million dollars.

I said people don't like stories about below-average days and people, but we're going to start way down here. Who is so low? It's a little girl. What's happened? Her mother has died, and her father has remarried a vile-tempered, ugly woman with two nasty daughters. Anyway, there's a party at the palace that night. She can't go. She has to help everybody else get ready. Now, does she sink lower? No. She's a staunch little girl, and she has had the maximum whack from fate, which is the loss of her mother. She can't go any lower than that.

CINDERELLA

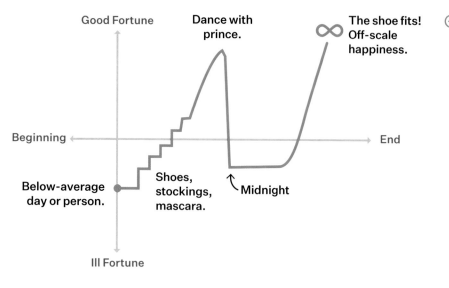

Vonnegut, writing in his autobiography *Palm Sunday*, found a similarity between the Cinderella story arc and arcs within the Christian Bible:

"The stroke of midnight looked exactly like the unique creation myth in the Old Testament. And the rise to bliss at the end was identical with the expectation of redemption, as expressed in primitive Christianity. The tales were identical."

This shape is the most popular in Western storytelling, and the most similar to Joseph Campbell's classic, *The Hero's Journey*.

Okay, so the fairy godmother comes, gives her shoes, gives her stockings, gives her mascara, gives her a means of transportation. She goes to the party, dances with the prince, has a swell time.

Boing, boing, boing—now there's a slight inclination to that line as I've drawn it, because it takes perhaps 20 seconds, 30 seconds for a grandfather clock to strike 12. Does she wind up at the same level? Of course not. She will remember that dance for the rest of her life. Now she poops along on this level until the prince comes, the shoe fits, and she achieves off-scale happiness."[28]

Vonnegut's shape for the Cinderella story is very close to the structure of Joseph Campbell's *The Hero's Journey*. In Campbell's research, he uncovered a common structure of mythical proportions in the religions and cultural stories of Eastern and Western cultures. The struggle is harder, the hero works harder, and the victory is greater. When a story is told in this format, it hits a cultural nerve unlike any other. Western cultures tend to prefer stories with a happy ending. Most blockbuster movies conform to this shape due to how decisively the hero is redeemed from hardship.

Data Confirms an Emotional Arc in Stories

Vonnegut's wish for a computer to process story shapes came true in 2016, when a team of data scientists at the Computational Story Lab at the University of Vermont unveiled an impressive research project. They had a computer analyze 1,327 digitized works of fiction from the Gutenberg Project.[29]

To discover the emotional arcs of the stories, the researchers used sentiment analysis, which tracks the rise and fall of positive and negative emotions in a piece of text. They then broke the stories down into distinct emotional arcs, which ended in either good or bad fortune.

The analysis produced the six main emotional arcs shown over the next few pages. The first set of three (to the right) end in good fortune, and on the following pages, you'll find three ending in ill fortune.

This team was the first to create empirical evidence of how closely stories conform to the axes as Vonnegut summarized them.

If the charts on the next couple of pages represented business results, they would be recognizable to you, because many organizations experience ill fortune and good fortune over time. These bar charts conform to the same patterns in the six story arcs.

If you have a chart that ends in good fortune, you can reveal each bar (or line segment) one at a time. When revealing one statistic at a time, the outcome is inconclusive to the audience until the final bit of data is revealed. This sets up suspense in the audience until they know definitively that it ends with a positive resolution.

DATA ENDING IN GOOD FORTUNE

RAGS TO RICHES

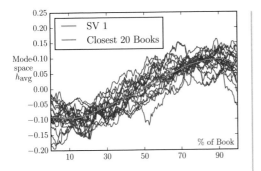

Steady Rise

Alice's Adventures Underground, Dream, and *The Ballad of Reading Gaol.*

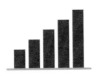

MAN IN A HOLE

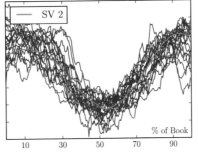

Fall-Rise

The Magic of Oz, Teddy Bears, The Autobiography of St. Ignatius, and *Typhoon.*

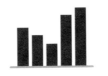

CINDERELLA

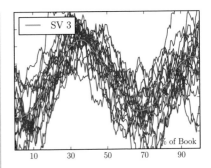

Rise-Fall-Rise

Cinderella, A Christmas Carol, Sophist, and *The Consolation of Philosophy.*[30]

Notice how the three charts above end in good fortune. By presenting these charts over time, you can create suspense of impending ill fortune, and when it resolves positively, this can create a sense of elation in the audience.

Data Confirms an Emotional Arc in Stories *(continued)*

DATA ENDING IN ILL FORTUNE

TRAGEDY

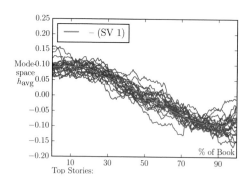

Steady Fall

Romeo and Juliet, The House of the Vampire, Savrola, and *The Dance.*

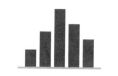

ICARUS

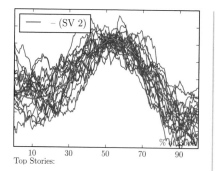

Rise-Fall

Icarus, Stories from Hans Christian Andersen, The Rome Express, and *The Yoga Sutras of Patanjali.*

OEDIPUS

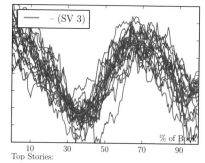

Fall-Rise-Fall

Oedipus Rex, On the Nature of Things, The Wonder Book of Bible Stories, and *A Hero of Our Time.*

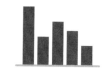

The three charts above end in ill fortune. Sometimes, ill fortune is the final outcome ending in tragedy. At other times, the audience still has time to change their behavior to reshape the ending of your DataStory.

If your organization has experienced a swing from good fortune to ill fortune, the shape of the charts on the left may look all too familiar.

In classic literature, stories ending in ill fortune usually feature a character of great stature or promise with a character flaw. When a crisis tests their character, they succumb to the flaw and die—figuratively or literally. Caesar's flaw was ambition, Romeo's flaw was his impulsiveness, and Icarus and Oedipus both had pride as their flaw.

When presenting data ending in ill fortune, you must know the cause. It may be due to executing a project in a flawed way, but more likely, it is a flaw in strategy or management. Know the cause, own it, and address it directly and emphatically.

ENDING IN ILL FORTUNE

If all financial and human effort cannot turn around the outcome of the data, make that very clear so your audience can process the finality of it. Ending in ill fortune makes an audience feel pity or fear for those who have lost their struggle. They experience catharsis by learning from the mistakes of those who have lost.

REVERSAL OF FORTUNE

What if your current data shows ill fortune, but there is time for the people in the audience to change the outcome? Help them see their role as the hero helping to overcome an adversary, and inspire them to feel it's doable.

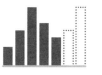

Let's say your current performance follows the Icarus rise-fall pattern, but there's still time to change the outcome.

The way you communicate can make obstacles and adversaries seem surmountable.

TIP ▶ Go to duarte.com/datastory to find Vonnegut's lecture as well as a link to the research on the six basic shapes, the hedonometer, and an interactive visualization tool of all the story data.

Reverse Ill Fortune into a Cinderella Arc
Case Study: Internal All-Hands Meeting

Below is a series of slides a CEO of a medium-sized business delivered at an internal all-hands meeting.

She retold the story of the difficult journey her employees had been on over the past few years, and ended by revealing the final heroic improvement they had achieved.

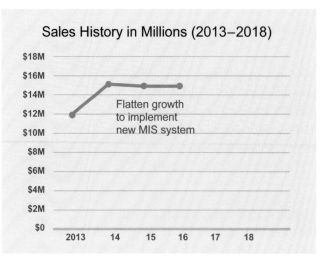

1   The CEO explained how it'd been a tough few years as they put in a new company brain (MIS system). During that season, she had approved revenue staying flat because driving that much change while also trying to grow would have brought employees to their knees.

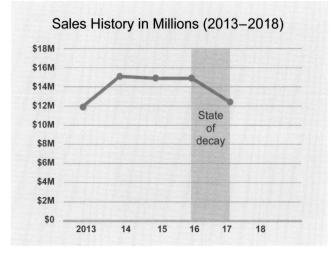

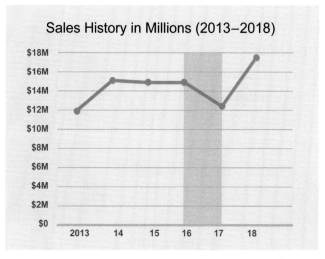

(2) In 2016, the company lurched downward into what she called a "state of decay." Swapping out the company brain had frayed nerves and created strain around data integrity. The company turned on itself, and wasn't productive.

(3) In early 2017, the team recommitted to their core values and instituted clear initiatives for digging out of the pit, and when she did her big reveal showing the stellar final numbers, the employees erupted.

Charity: Water Storytelling with Data
Case Study: Scott Harrison

Scott Harrison has an enviable operating model among nonprofit CEOs. He curated an exclusive group of individuals and organizations called The Well, and this group funds all operational and overhead expenses. By having all of his OpEx covered by this group, he can make a promise to all individual donors that 100 percent of their money will go to building wells that bring people clean water.

Each year, he hosts a dinner so members of The Well can see the impact. In his 2018 speech, he connected the audience with the data beautifully.

"Some of you have been following our trajectory from the very beginning.

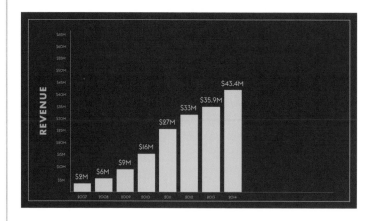

We grew every year. We grew through downturns, we grew when other charities were shrinking. We had eight years of consecutive growth. That's just what we did: grow. And then, in 2015, we experienced what it was like to shrink.

It was TERRIBLE. It began an awful existential crisis for me. For me, and for the team.

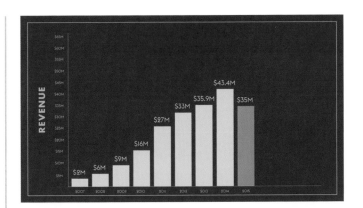

These numbers aren't money in our pocket. We're not buying cars or houses with it. It's for people to get clean water. So we went from getting one million people clean water in year eight to only 820,000 the next year.

Ⓐ **Humanize the Characters**
Harrison consistently converts the amount of money into the quantity of people with clean water, reminding the audience of why they give.

What happened? We had two huge gifts that didn't repeat due to market conditions.

We realized we needed to fix this problem, because we had so little repeatability in our organization when it came to donations. So we came up with the idea of The Spring, a subscription service with a model similar to the way Netflix, DropBox, and Spotify are growing their businesses.

Thirty dollars a month can give one person clean water. And we invited people to give to clean water every month with this powerful promise that 100 percent of what they gave would go directly to people in need of clean water.

I think we were surprised at how quickly it grew around the world, thanks to a 20-minute video we made. We launched it at the end of that year, and saw just a little bit of growth in 2016.

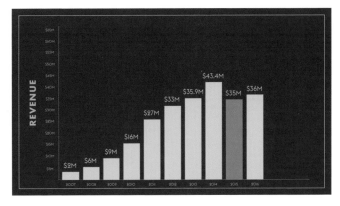

But then we had 40 percent growth in 2017, and our first $50 million year—demonstrating the benefit of a growing
subscription program.

<applause>

And last year, we got 1.2 million people clean water.

Storytelling with Data (Cinderella)
Harrison revealed the chart and narrative over time. As with Vonnegut's emotional arc of *Cinderella*, the audience wasn't sure if the ill fate would turn around.
This is the most popular Western story structure.

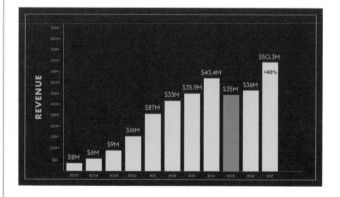

And the numbers Lauren had in her earlier presentation are already old, and they were only from a month ago.

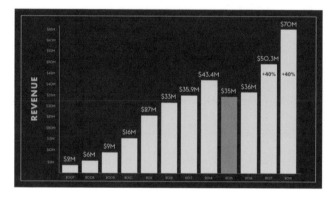

This year, we are trending toward $70 million.

<uproar>

Surprised by the Unexpected
Whether it was intentional or not, Harrison's audience had already seen a lower number earlier in the presentation, and then he showed a much higher number than expected. In response, the audience gasped and then roared with applause.

Just to put this growth into perspective for a second, this is not what we are seeing among our counterparts. In fact, what we are hearing is that 'flat is the new up.'

"FLAT IS THE NEW UP"

Charitable giving to the international sector
declined by 6% from 2016 to 2017

Last year, giving declined 6 percent. International giving was net negative 6 percent, and we grew 40 percent. We're really excited about the work we've done for 12 years, and subscriptions are working."

⊙ **Attach Context to Data**

When context about the performance of other nonprofits is revealed, the audience realizes this is an even larger victory.

Later in the talk, Harrison employed additional methods to connect the audience to the data.

"This is always my favorite stat, which is the number of people we're giving clean water every day. It's been fun to see this go up every year.

Think about that. Today, 4000 brand-new people got clean water for the first time. I was at Madison Square Garden recently for a sold out Depeche Mode concert. I looked online to see how many people fit in the arena. I turned to my wife and said, 'You know, we give water to this many people every four days!'

⬆ **Marvel at the Magnitude**
For the audience to understand the number of people receiving clean water every day, Harrison connected the audience to something familiar. Madison Square Garden holds close to 20,000 people for a concert.

That's really our KPI. We want that number to go up, and go up faster, so we're able to bring more people from dirty water to clean.

We asked the question: What would it take to be even more ambitious, to think about growing even faster? What would it take to reach 25 million more people by the year 2025?

That's a lot of people. That is 1,000 Oracle Arenas, it's 28 times the number of people who live here in San Francisco, and it's three times the population of New York City. So that feels like an even more significant impact. And again, it's all about these individual lives.

(▲) **Marvel at the Magnitude**
Harrison has a huge vision to dramatically increase the number of people with access to clean water. He again uses relatable spaces full of people to convey how many people will get clean water.

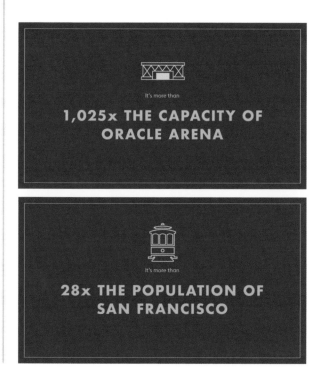

You will hear us constantly coming back to the individuals we're serving, like this woman, Aberhat.

She is a 47-year-old mother of four; she is a wife. She is walking four to six hours every single day to get the most disgusting water you've ever seen. And she has no other option. These are the conditions she was born in to. And we know how to help her."

(▲) **Humanize the Characters**
The audience is shown a photo of Aberhat, a woman whose life has been changed by clean water. Harrison explains that the next night at the annual gala, The Well members will be immersed in a 360-degree presentation about how her life has been transformed.

"Each day holds a surprise. But only if we expect it can we see, hear, or feel it when it comes to us. Let's not be afraid to receive each day's surprise, whether it comes to us as sorrow or as joy. It will open a new place in our hearts, a place where we can welcome new friends and celebrate more fully our shared humanity."

HENRI NOUWEN
PRIEST, AUTHOR, AND PROFESSOR

Almost everything can be counted and measured. It's thrilling to treasure-hunt through data and uncover bytes of golden opportunity or cures for many of life's ills. We are only in the formative phase of the ways in which data will change our lives, and it needs the help of a communicator. **Transforming numbers into narratives will become part of every leader's job.**

We rely on data to tell us what has happened, and stories to tell us what it means. Stories frame data so decisions can be made faster and inspire others to take action by changing their hearts and minds. **Words are powerful. Skillfully wielding them only comes with practice.**

As you journey through your career, **may you master the science of data, and also the art of communicating it.**

APPENDIX

Move the Narrative Forward

The most common conjunctions are *but*, *and*, or *so*. Below is a guide of other conjunctions you can use to knit together a three-act DataStory (see page 65).

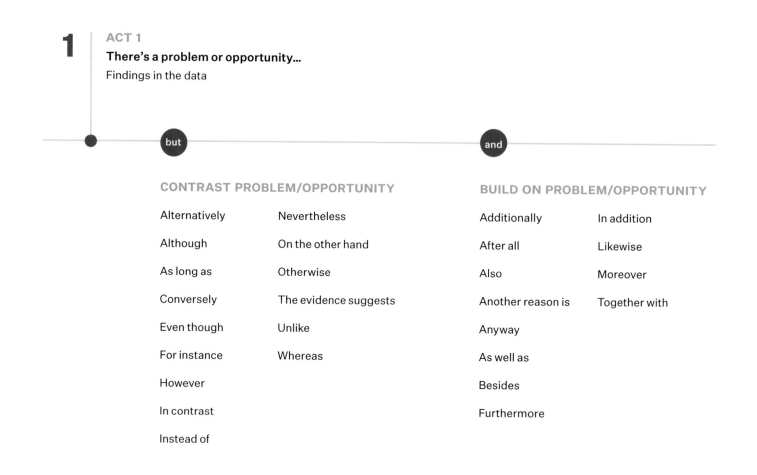

1   ACT 1

There's a problem or opportunity...
Findings in the data

but

and

CONTRAST PROBLEM/OPPORTUNITY

Alternatively	Nevertheless
Although	On the other hand
As long as	Otherwise
Conversely	The evidence suggests
Even though	Unlike
For instance	Whereas
However	
In contrast	
Instead of	

BUILD ON PROBLEM/OPPORTUNITY

Additionally	In addition
After all	Likewise
Also	Moreover
Another reason is	Together with
Anyway	
As well as	
Besides	
Furthermore	

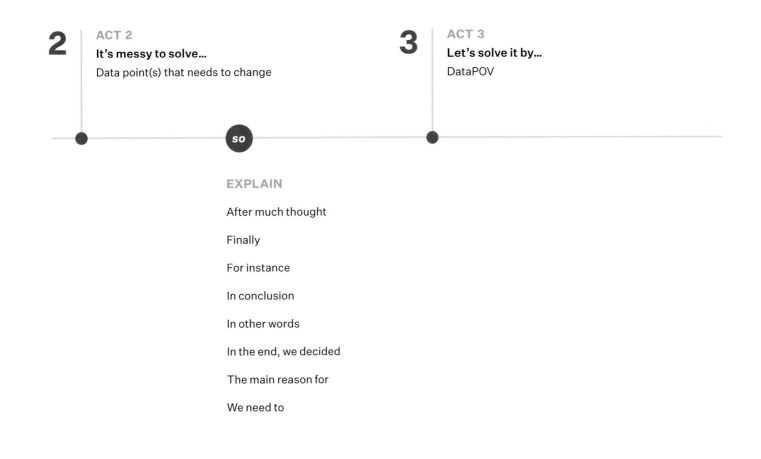

2 | ACT 2
It's messy to solve...
Data point(s) that needs to change

so

3 | ACT 3
Let's solve it by...
DataPOV

EXPLAIN

After much thought

Finally

For instance

In conclusion

In other words

In the end, we decided

The main reason for

We need to

Speed Up Decision-Making with a One-Page Recommendation Tree

Sometimes, a recommendation needs pages of supporting evidence. At other times, a one-pager will do. A one-pager can be distributed in a meeting, sent via email, or used as a conversation piece to review with a decision-maker.

TACTICAL EXAMPLE

Digital marketers identified through data that the checkout experience was hurting their sales.

Recommendation Tree from a Marketing Manager   **D**

EXECUTIVE SUMMARY

ACT 1	ACT 2	ACT 3 (DataPOV)
Even though we got **2x** the amount of anticipated traffic to our site, we didn't meet our first-year revenue goal.	**74%** of our potential customers abandoned their shopping carts.	Changing the shopping cart experience and shipping policies could increase sales by **40%**.

ACTION PLAN

	ACT 1	ACT 2	ACT 3
WHAT	**Implement** optional registration.	**Design** "Save Cart" functionality.	**Offer** free shipping for all orders over $50.
WHY	**28%** of users abandon their shopping carts because they do not want to register.	**37%** of shoppers are just browsing and comparison shopping. Let's make it easy for them to complete the purchase.	**56%** of shoppers leave because of unexpected costs. Shipping is the most frequently cited cost.
HOW	• **Expand** functionality to include a "Guest" purchasing option.	• **Prioritize** developers to build "Save Cart" functionality. • **Leverage** their interest by deploying email reminders.	• **Start** providing free shipping on orders over $50 where profit margin is minimally impacted. • **Reengage** former buyers through new shipping model via email campaign.

© Duarte Press, LLC | www.duarte.com/datastory

TIP ▶ Go online for a free one-page Recommendation Tree template at duarte.com/datastory.

STRATEGIC EXAMPLE

An IT director whose team is crippled by outdated infrastructure loses sleep over a potential security breach and the rising costs of maintaining the current system. On page 136, this was built out as an entire Slidedoc.[31]

Recommendation Tree from an IT Director   **D**

EXECUTIVE SUMMARY

ACT 1	ACT 2	ACT 3 (DataPOV)
Our legacy technology systems are highly complex and disparate. These systems provide little visibility into analytics across the entire ecosystem. They also cannot protect us against security threats.	Maintaining outdated technology and protecting it against security threats drives our annual operating costs higher than most companies our size. Frustrations with these legacy systems have led to high turnover within the IT department.	Redesigning IT infrastructure into a cloud-based system will secure our teams, data, and costs.

ACTION PLAN

WHAT	Reduce complexities of disconnected systems.	Focus IT efforts on new systems implementation.	Integrate security with a cloud-based solution.
WHY	It's costly and difficult to manage multiple technology systems. An integrated, cloud-based approach will collect analytics that enable better insights across all systems.	Our top IT managers spend the majority of their time overseeing the help desk. They are qualified to drive this implementation, and would be energized by the new challenge.	With an integrated security solution, we can ensure our new technology systems are protected from sophisticated outside threats.
HOW	• **Implement** a consolidated cloud-based systems approach. • **Migrate** existing data into new, unified system. • **Audit** software service offerings and opt-in to subscriptions as needed.	• **Identify** top talent to run implementation project to minimize consulting fees. • **Shift** help-desk queries to a lower-cost, third-party vendor. • **Require** IT training on new systems to optimize capabilities.	• **Craft** data-governance protocol; design a new security policy to mitigate risk. • **Create** an incident response plan.

REFERENCES

INTRODUCTION

1   Pamela Rutledge, "The Psychological Power of Storytelling," Psychology Today, January 16, 2011.

2   Lauri Nnummenmaa, et al. "Emotional Speech Synchronizes Brains Across Listeners and Engages Large-Scale Dynamic Brain Networks," Neuroimage, November 15, 2014.

3   Jennifer Edson Escalas, "Imagine Yourself in the Product: Mental Stimulation, Narrative Transportation, and Persuasion," Journal of Advertising (2004).

4   Paul Zak, "Empathy, Neurochemistry, and the Dramatic Arc," YouTube video, posted February 19, 2013, https://www.youtube.com/watch?v=DHeqQAKHh3M.

5   Chip Heath, Dan Heath, "Made to Stick: Why Some Ideas Survive and Others Die" (New York: Random House, 2007, 2008).

6   "Writing Skills Matter, Even for Numbers-Crunching Big Data Jobs," Burning Glass Technologies, September 11, 2017, https://www.burning-glass.com/blog/writing-skills-big-data-jobs/.

CHAPTER I: BECOMING A COMMUNICATOR OF DATA

7   John Gantz, David Reinsel, John Rydning. "The Digitization of the World, From Edge to Core," Seagate/IDC, https://www.seagate.com/files/www-content/our-story/trends/files/idc-seagatedataage-whitepaper.pdf.

8   "What's Next for the Data Science and Analytics Job Market?" PwC, https://www.pwc.com/us/en/library/data-science-and-analytics.html.

9   Josh Bersin, "Catch the Wave: The 21st-century Career," Deloitte Review, July 13, 2017, https://www2.deloitte.com/insights/us/en/deloitte-review/issue-21/changing-nature-of-careers-in-21st-century.html.

10   Marissa Mayer, "How to Make the Star Employees You Need," Masters of Scale, https://mastersofscale.com/marissa-mayer-how-to-make-the-star-employees-you-need-masters-of-scale-podcast/.

CHAPTER II: COMMUNICATING TO DECISION-MAKERS

11   Sujan Patel, "Daily Routines of Fortune 500 Leaders (and What You Can Learn from Them)," Zirtual, August 18, 2016, https://blog.zirtual.com/how-fortune-500-leaders-schedule-their-days.

12   James Kosur, "17 Business Leaders on Integrating Work and Life," World Economic Forum, November 23, 2015, https://www.weforum.org/agenda/2015/11/17-business-leaders-on-integrating-work-and-life/.

13   Shellye Archambeau, "Phase 2," January 3, 2018, https://shellyearchambeau.com/blog/2018/1/1/phase-2-7n5gw.

14   Kathleen Elkins, "14 Time-management Tricks from Richard Branson and Other Successful People," CNBC, February 17, 2017, https://www.cnbc.com/2017/02/17/time-management-tricks-from-richard-branson-other-successful-people.html.

CHAPTER V: CREATING ACTION THROUGH ANALYTICAL STRUCTURE

15   George Miller, "Observations on the Faltering Progression of Science," https://www.ncbi.nlm.nih.gov/pubmed/25751370.

16   "Assumptions for Statistical Tests," Real Statistics Using Excel, http://www.real-statistics.com/descriptive-statistics/assumptions-statistical-test/.

17   Claire Cain Miller, "The Number of Female Chief Executives Is Falling," The New York Times, May 23, 2018, https://www.nytimes.com/2018/05/23/upshot/why-the-number-of-female-chief-executives-is-falling.html.

CHAPTER IX: MARVELING AT THE MAGNITUDE

18   Tweet: https://twitter.com/neiltyson/status/995095196760092672.

19   Hillary Hoffower, Shayanne Gal, "We Did the Math to Calculate Exactly How Much Billionaires and Celebrities Like Jeff Bezos and Kylie Jenner Make an Hour," Business Insider, August 26, 2018, https://www.businessinsider.in/we-did-the-math-to-calculate-exactly-how-much-money-billionaires-and-celebrities-like-jeff-bezos-and-kylie-jenner-make-per-hour/articleshow/65552498.cms.

20   Eric Collins, "How Many Bacteria Are in the Ocean?" August 25, 2009, http://www.reric.org/wordpress/archives/648.

21   Kevin Loria, "The Giant Garbage Vortex in the Pacific Ocean Is Over Twice the Size of Texas—Here's What It Looks Like," Business Insider, September 8, 2018, https://www.businessinsider.com/greatpacific-garbage-patch-view-study-plastic-2018-3.

22   Apple.com, iPhone 6S Environmental Report, https://www.apple.com/environment/pdf/products/iphone/iPhone6s_PER_sept2015.pdf.

23   Len Fisher, "If You Could Drive a Car Upwards at 60 mph, How Long Would It Take to Get to the Moon?" Science Focus, https://www.sciencefocus.com/space/if-you-could-drive-a-car-upwards-at-60mph-how-long-would-it-take-to-get-to-the-moon/.

24   Jesper Sanders, "100+ Exclamations: The Ultimate Interjection List," Survey Anyplace Blog, March 23, 2017, https://surveyanyplace.com/the-ultimate-interjection-list/.

25   Chris O' Brien, "TED 2013: 'Factivist' Bono Projects Poverty Rate of Zero by 2030," Los Angeles Times, February 26, 2013, https://www.latimes.com/business/la-xpm-2013-feb-26-la-fi-tn-ted-2013-factivist-bono-projects-poverty-rate-of-zero-by-2030-20130226-story.html.

CHAPTER XI: STORYTELLING WITH DATA

26   Indeed data source: https://drive.google.com/drive/folders/1PmszxlVbtDP_npz5FMbkyOFnfg_s6U2O.

27   Stephen Galloway, "An Inconvenient Truth, 10 Years Later," The Hollywood Reporter, May 19, 2016, https://www.hollywoodreporter.com/features/an-inconvenient-truth-10-years-894691.

28   "Kurt Vonnegut on the Shapes of Stories," YouTube video, posted October 30, 2010, https://www.youtube.com/watch?v=oP3c1h8v2ZQ.

29   Andrew Reagan, "The Emotional Arcs of Stories Are Dominated by Six Basic Shapes," ArXiv, Cornell University, September 26, 2016, https://arxiv.org/abs/1606.07772.

30   Ronald Yates, "Study Says All Stories Conform to One of Six Plots," July 11, 2016, https://ronaldyatesbooks.com/2016/07/study-says-all-stories-conform-to-one-of-six-plots/.

31   SyberSafe, "A Data Breach May Be More Expensive Than You Think," July 20, 2018, https://sybersafe.com/2018/07/20/a-data-breach-may-be-more-expensive-than-you-think/.

PHOTO CREDITS

THANK YOU

Queen of Everything: Mary Ann Bologoff

Creative Direction: Jay Kapur

Art Direction: Fabian Espinoza, Diandra Macias

Design: Aisling Doyle

Cover Art: Jonathan Valiente

Editor: Emily Loose

Illustrations and Charts: Radha Joshi, Ivan Liberato,
Ryan Muta, Anna Ralston, Shane Tango

Production: Erin Casey, Theresa Jackson, Anna Ralston,
and Trami Truong

Annotations: Tyler Lynch

Proofing: David Little, Emily Williams

Case Study: Kate Devlin, Xiddia Gonzalez

Photo Credits: Dan Gard, Ryan Orcutt

Special Thanks: Trisha Bailey, Chariti Canny,
Dr. R. Joseph Childs, Donna Duarte, Michael Duarte,
Kevin Friesen, Megan Huston, Mike Pacchione,
and Kerry Rodden

INDEX

HERE

HERE

HERE

HERE

HERE

HERE

THERE

Move your audience from *here* to *there*.

Everyone has an idea worth sharing, but not everyone has the natural ability to communicate it well. With Duarte's unique blend of strategy, story, visualization, and coaching, we can help you change hearts and minds.

Duarte, Inc. has spent decades creating presentations for top brands. As we've mastered the art of communicating, we have codified our principles into training to teach you, your team, or your entire company to become stronger communicators using empathy-based, VisualStory® techniques.

The Duarte Method™ teaches you how to shape your ideas into a cohesive story, amplify them with purposeful visuals, and adapt your delivery to better connect with your audience—**all with empathy at the core.**

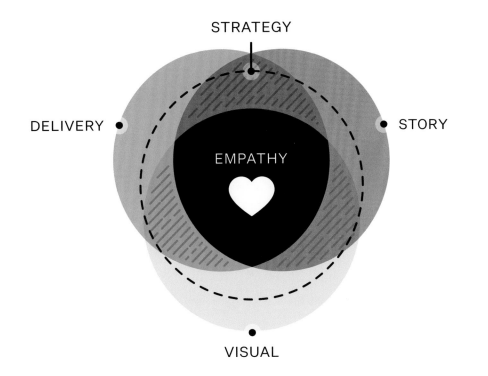

STRATEGY

DELIVERY

STORY

EMPATHY

VISUAL

Slidedocs®

Download this practical book with templates and an online course. Learn how information-rich slides can spread ideas— no formal presentation necessary.

Slide Design Lab

Learn to build sleek slides in PowerPoint® the way the pros do. Pick up skills to improve your slide design—and your productivity—immediately.

Our books, courses, and coaching can help you communicate best.

Slide:ology

De-clutter slides and simplify complex concepts by turning words into pictures and building slides with clear visual messages.

Resonate

Apply lessons from story and cinema to structure content into a persuasive presentation that grabs your audience's attention and influences them to act.

DataStory

Data is a science; communicating it is an art. Write a recommendation and inspire others by applying storytelling principles when sharing data insights.

Captivate

Command the room with speaker coaching and executive presence training. Our approach leverages your authentic strengths to improve your speaking style and delivery.

HBR Guide

Learn presentation fundamentals for creating your content, visualizing it, and then delivering it in an engaging way. This popular course is based on the best-selling book many business schools use.

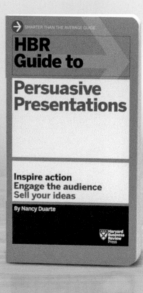

Illuminate

Transformation is hard, but story can ease the path forward. This award-winning book and experiential workshop equips leaders with empathetic communication tools to guide people on the journey of change.

LeaderStory

Encourage leaders to recall, construct, and authentically share their most important stories with an immersive workshop experience.

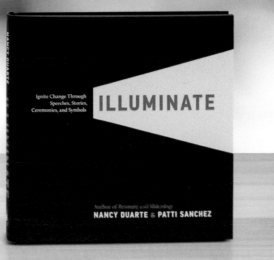

Free Downloadable Goodies Referenced in DataStory

Slidedoc Book and Templates
Free book and professionally built templates you can modify to fit your brand.

One-Page Recommendation Tree
If your recommendation is on the tactical side, use this simple format.

Annotation Kit
This kit of cool shapes to overlay on your charts will save you time.

Animated Charts
Clever animated examples of charts for you to download and deconstruct.

Go to **duarte.com/datastory**